A RATIONAL APPROACH

TO

JUDAISM

AND

TORAH COMMENTARY

Other books by Israel Drazin:

Targumic Studies
Targum Onkelos to Exodus
Targum Onkelos to Leviticus
Targum Onkelos to Numbers
Targum Onkelos to Deuteronomy

Editor of:
Living Legends

With Cecil B. Currey:
For God and Country

With Stanley Wagner:
Onkelos on the Torah: Understanding the Bible Text – Genesis
Onkelos on the Torah: Understanding the Bible Text – Exodus

A RATIONAL APPROACH

TO

JUDAISM

AND

TORAH COMMENTARY

Israel Drazin

URIM PUBLICATIONS
Jerusalem • New York

A Rational Approach to Judaism and Torah Commentary
by Israel Drazin

First Edition.
ISBN 965-7108-91-8

Urim Publications, P.O. Box 52287, Jerusalem 91521 Israel

Lambda Publishers Inc.
3709 13th Avenue Brooklyn, New York 11218 U.S.A.
Tel: 718-972-5449 Fax: 718-972-6307
E-mail: mh@ejudaica.com

www.UrimPublications.com

Dedicated
to
my wife
Dina Drazin

Acknowledgements

There were quite a few people who inspired me to write this book and I deeply appreciate their inspirations. I want to thank my friends, Rabbis Stanley M. Wagner, Benjamin Roth, Shamma Friedman, Simcha Freedman, Leonard Small and Zvi Yehuda, as well as the groups I met with on Friday nights and Saturday for the Shabbat meals, and the dozens who attend my Tuesday morning classes, Stuart Harris with whom I study on Thursdays, and Dr. Raphi Jospe with whom I meet and talk when I am in Israel. I also want to thank my children who helped me in various ways, Daniela Shoshana Levin, Michele Malka Lenoff, Sarena Leba Lieder and Stephen Allan Drazin. Special thanks to Rochel U. Berman, the noted author of *Dignity Beyond Death* who was a constant source of ideas, and to Sue Lowenkron who suggested that I write this book.

CONTENTS

Introduction

This book rejects the notion that religious people must avoid using their intellect, live in the past, steer clear of personal and social progress, focus every moment and thought on life after death and shun the goods of this world. These people do not understand the truth and value of religion.

The ancient Sadducees, a Jewish faction that flourished in the last centuries B.C.E and vanished when the second Temple was destroyed by the Romans in 70 C.E., misunderstood the biblical command prohibiting fire in homes on the Sabbath. They assumed that God demanded that they pass the seventh day secluded in dark and cold houses. Their opponents, the Pharisees, the ancestors of Rabbinic Judaism, clarified that the Bible prohibited igniting a fire, but allowed and even encouraged the use of the glow and warmth of the flame. They invented the concept to light Shabbat candles before the advent of the holy day – and highlighted the ritual with a blessing – to stress that Judaism teaches exactly the opposite lesson.

A young lady gave birth to a boy. Her father was overjoyed.

"When and where will you have the circumcision?" he asked.

"We won't have one," she said.

"Why? This is a basic Jewish practice. How can my grandchild not be circumcised! You have to do it!"

"No we don't! It is barbaric and pagan!"

"But this is what identifies us as Jews! I don't understand your attitude."

"Look papa, God is perfect and everything that He made is perfect. Isn't it wrong, indeed arrogant, for us to destroy what God made perfectly?"

"You're missing the point. Sure God is perfect, but He made humans in a way that teaches them that they, the humans, are not perfect – that they have a duty to complete what God started – that they must create just as God created. Circumcision is an example. Every time that we circumcise a boy, we should realize that we have a responsibility to perfect ourselves and the world."

This book presents a rational approach to Judaism and the Torah. It is designed to stimulate thinking and to teach us how to improve ourselves and the world. Rationalists base their actions on reason and knowledge rather than on an emotional or passive response. They realize that they dare not do nothing, that they have a responsibility to improve.

This book will address provocative questions such as:

What does God require of people?

Is having faith blindly following what God demands, or does He want us to question?

How should we interpret the Bible?

How do we deal with seemingly unreasonable midrashic stories?

Does God want us to pray?

What is the value of the Synagogue?

Do Jews believe in angels and, if not, what do they mean to us?

Do current rabbis behave like the ancient rabbis?

How did the rabbinical sermon start and what should it accomplish?

What is the value of comparing biblical stories to Greek myths?

Are we obligated to accept the truth when it is taught by a non-Jew?

The book will reveal surprising facts, such as:

Passover does not occur when we think it does.

Opinions differ even among traditional scholars and rabbis as to whether Moses wrote the entire Five Books of Moses and whether God participated in the writing of the book of Deuteronomy.

Famous and respected Jewish scholars and rabbis believed in the involvement of demons in the everyday affairs of people and explained certain biblical verses and practices based on this belief.

Some Bible commentators were convinced that magic and astrology works and that the Bible verifies this truth.

In short, the goal of this volume is to inform its readers of facts that are generally withheld from them, to prompt the readers to think and to improve.

"When I die," said the Chassidic Rebbe Susya, "God will not say to me, 'Susya, why weren't you like Abraham, Isaac and Jacob?' Nor will He say to me, 'Susya, why weren't you like Moses?' He will say, "Susya, why weren't you as good as you, Susya, could have been?"'

Bereishit

What does God want from us?

Books generally open with an introduction that summarizes the essence of the contents for the reader. The opening of the Pentateuch, the first chapters of *Genesis,* can be understood as such an introduction. Verses 1:26 states, "Let us make man in our *demut.* Verse 1:27 relates that "God made man in His *tzelem,* in the *tzelem* of God, He made him."

Questions
1. If chapter 1 of *Genesis* is an introduction to the rest of the Bible, what is it telling us?
2. Do the words *demut* and *tzelem* tell us what constitutes a human being and what God expects from humans?
3. Should the biblical narratives and laws be interpreted based on the idea presented in the introduction?

God wants people to use their intelligence: The views of non-Jews
The American satirist Ambrose Bierce (1842–c. 1913) defined man in his humorous *The Devil's Dictionary* as, "An animal so lost in rapturous contemplation of what he thinks he is as to overlook what he indubitably ought to be."

The highly influential Greek rational philosopher Aristotle (384–322 B.C.E.), in his *Politics* and *Metaphysics* and other writings, wrote on this subject. He explained that the thing that makes a human being different than the beast is his intelligence. Therefore, if a person wants to be human he must use his intelligence – know all that he can know – otherwise he is little different than a beast.

Aristotle's teacher Plato (427–347) was more emphatic in his *Alcibiades I.* He described knowledge as the part of a person that "resembles God." Both

Plato and Aristotle were familiar with the injunction inscribed atop the Greek temple of Delphi, "Know thyself."

The opinion of Maimonides

The great Jewish rational philosopher Moses Maimonides (1138–1204), in his *Guide of the Perplexed,* agreed with these views and expanded upon them. It is not only rational that human beings must use their intelligence, this is what God demands. God does not want people to vegetate or live a passive life.

In the first chapter of the *Guide,* Maimonides writes that a literal meaning of the word *demut* is "likeness." This literal meaning may lead a person to suppose that God is saying that He wants to make man in His "likeness." But this is obviously not the Bible's intention. God has no body, and man can not have God's "likeness." Similarly, the literal meaning of *tzelem* is "shape" or "form." And again it is impossible to suppose that God made man with His divine "shape."

Maimonides therefore concludes that the terms "likeness" and "form" refer to the essence of a thing. The essence is that which differentiates one thing from everything else. The essence of a human is his intelligence. It is his intelligence that distinguishes him from animals. Thus, the introductory statements of the Bible are stating that people were given intelligence. Maimonides writes:

> As man's distinction consists in a property that no other earthly creature possesses, intellectual perception…this perception has been compared – as being similar to, but not actually like – the divine perception, which needs no corporeal organ.

Biblical support for this interpretation

The command to use one's intelligence also appears in *Deuteronomy* 10:12–13. God says: "And now Israel, what does the Lord require of you: only to fear the Lord your God, to walk in His ways, and to love Him, and serve the Lord your God with all your heart and with all your being, to keep the commands of the Lord and His statutes, which I command you this day for your good."

Maimonides recognizes that the concepts of "love" and "fear" in relation to God are meaningless because "love" and "fear" are emotions that are generally expressed in a passive fashion and they do not prompt man to act. He interprets the command as "come to know God." This means that we are required to develop our mind as best we can to know God and His creations.

Maimonides sees this command to use one's intelligence in other biblical verses as well, such as *Deuteronomy* 6:5, "You shall love the Lord your God with all your heart."

Other support for this interpretation

The rabbinically accepted Aramaic translation of the Pentateuch *Targum Onkelos*, composed around the year 400 C.E., highlights the idea that man's distinctive characteristic is his speech and intelligence. It paraphrases *Genesis* 2:7: "The Lord God formed man of the dust of the ground, and breathed into his nostrils the breath of life; and man became a *nefesh chayah.*"

Onkelos does not render the latter phrase as "a living being," but uses the opportunity to inform us of man's distinctive characteristic, *ruach m'mal'la*, "one with the power of speech," a phrase denoting a certain level of intelligence.

This targumic interpretation can be traced to the beginning of the Common Era when the Egyptian Jewish philosopher Philo identified "the breath of life" with human rationality in his *Specialibus Legibus* 4:123.

The concept of "wisdom" was so important in early Judaism that the Aramaic Bible translation called *Neophyti*, dated by some scholars to the beginning of the Common Era, begins its rendering of *Genesis* by stating that in the beginning God created the world "with wisdom."

Applying the idea of the use of intelligence to the interpretation of Scripture

In the introduction to his Bible commentary, the rationalist commentator Abraham ibn Ezra (1089–1164) states that there are several approaches to the interpretation of the Bible. He wrote that he opted for the rationalistic approach, clarifying the text by using his intelligence rather than relying on fanciful midrashic elaborations that contain ideas that may not even be hinted in the biblical text. However, he added, when the rational approach contradicts the Rabbinic teaching of law, he opts for the latter.

The rationalistic Bible commentator Rashbam (c. 1080–1168) also wrote in his commentary to *Genesis* 37:2 about the need to use one's intelligence in understanding the plain meaning of the scriptural text. He tells us that even his grandfather, the famous and popular commentator Rashi, admitted that this is a good way of understanding the text. After explaining his rationalistic method of Bible interpretation to his grandfather, Rashbam states that "he admitted to me that if he had time, he would have composed additional commentaries that would [not concentrate as he had done on midrashic interpretation, but] focus on the plain meanings that are discovered daily."

Summary

The first chapter of the Bible can be seen as an introduction that informs people that they have intelligence and are obligated to use it. This concept was recognized by non-Jews, including the famous ancient Greek philosophers. Maimonides found this concept in the words *tzelem* and *demut*. He interpreted other parts of the Bible as reminders of the same message. His understanding of the first chapter was supported by many other Jewish sources, before his time and afterwards. Since humans are required to use their intelligence, rational Bible commentators insisted that Scripture should be examined carefully with this in mind.

*   *   *

The life unexamined is not worth living for a human being.
        –Plato, *Apology*

God gave man an upright countenance (with the duty) to survey the heavens, and to look upward to the stars.
        –Ovid, *Metamorphoses*

Be all you can be.
        –Erich Fromm, *You Shall be as Gods*

Noach

Faith vs. Reason

Noah's generation acted perversely and God decided to destroy them. Noah was informed that the world would be flooded, but that he and his family would be saved. He was instructed to build an ark and he would float above the destructive waters. The Bible describes Noah as "a righteous man, perfect in his generation" (*Genesis* 6:9). He accepted God's decision, believed with calmness and quiet determination; he complied with every divine order without comment.

Questions
1. What is faith?
2. Did Noah use faith or reason?
3. Does it make sense for a person to rely on faith?
4. Did Noah act as a righteous man should act?
5. What is Maimonides' perspective on faith?

Definition of faith
Faith is the acceptance by a person that an idea is true even though his reasoning is unable to fully support its truthfulness. The American satirist Ambrose Bierce (1842–c. 1913) defined faith in his humorous *The Devil's Dictionary* as, "belief without evidence in what is told by one who speaks without knowledge of things without parallel."

Bierce defined religion based on faith sarcastically as, "A daughter of hope or fear, explaining to ignorance the nature of the unknowable."

Another unknown source wrote similarly, "Faith is believing what you know ain't so."

One can find other cynical comments in other sources. Each highlights the absence of any reasonable basis to faith and the difficulty that a person of faith has in making an informed decision. Unfortunately, most people resolve the decision difficulty by not thinking at all and by relying instead on the opinion of others.

Faith not mentioned in the Hebrew Bible

The term "faith" does not appear in the Hebrew Bible. Instead, the Bible frequently encourages one to think and to act reasonably. The biblical word that some mistakenly translate as "faith," *emunah*, actually means "steadfast" or "steady." Thus Moses held up his hands "steadily," without letting them fall.

The contrast between Abraham and Noah

Scripture paints contrasting portraits of two men, Abraham who used his reasoning ability and Noah who acted on blind faith.

In *Genesis* 18, Abraham listened to the divine decision to destroy the city of Sodom and other cities because of the evils that they committed. He reacted by debating the verdict with God. He demonstrated that one could, indeed should, reason and question even God about His resolutions. God approves of Abraham's behavior and acquiesces to his reasoning. God agrees that He will not destroy the cities if they contain ten righteous people.

Abraham's approach was followed by many biblical figures who questioned the reasonableness of divine communications. Moses, Isaiah and Jeremiah, for instance, argued that it was unreasonable for God to select them for His intended mission. The judge Gideon asked for proof after proof from God that he would be successful in fighting against what he thought were invincible Israelite foes. There is hardly any biblical figure that did not question the reasonableness of the act he was divinely sent to accomplish. These people used their intelligence as God wanted them to do.

In contrast, Noah hears a divine decree to destroy all living beings with a flood with silent acceptance. The Bible records no attempt by Noah to save the people and animals of his generation, and there is no reaction by him to the death of an entire civilization in the long story in *Genesis,* chapters 6–9. He accepted the divine decree and, based on his faith in God, allowed people to die. The only reaction recorded by Scripture is his loss of self control in getting drunk immediately after the flood. The Jewish historian Josephus (around 35–100 C.E.) was so bothered by Noah's "righteous" silence that he invented a dialogue between Noah and God in his imaginative recounting of the episode, in which Noah pleads with God after the flood not to bring another, and God agrees with his request.

Rabbis Judah and Nehemiah differed in the *Midrash Genesis Rabbah* whether Noah was really "righteous." Similarly, Rabbis Yohanan and Resh Lakish disagreed in the Babylonian Talmud, *Sanhedrin* 108a, in how to evaluate Noah. The former in each volume claimed that Noah was righteous only when he is compared with the people of his own generation. Rabbi Judah, for example, claimed, "In a street of totally blind people, a one-eyed man is called clear-sighted, and an infant a scholar." Rabbi Nehemiah took the opposite view. Noah "was like a tightly closed vial of perfume lying in a graveyard, which nevertheless gives out a fragrant odor, how much more sweetly it would smell if it were placed outside the graveyard."

However, even Rabbi Nehemiah admits Noah's limitations. Noah is describes in *Genesis* 6:9, as a man who "walked with God." The rabbi understands that Noah needed God's assistance as a crutch throughout his life. He was never humanly actualized. He deserved little credit for leaning on God for his faith and righteousness. Abraham, Rabbi Nehemiah admits, was different. *Genesis* 17:1 describes him as one who walks "before Me [God]." Abraham, says Rabbi Nehemiah, was like one who precedes God with a lantern showing people how to behave.

The two sages do not differ on whether Noah acted in an ideal manner. They agree that he did not. If Noah had acted correctly, everyone would have agreed that he was righteous. However, the sages who felt he was righteous would have to agree with the *Mishnah, Pirke Avot* 2:6 that states: "An individual who acts without reason can still be a righteous fool. "

Maimonides

Moses Maimonides (1138–1204) repeatedly stressed that people should not accept ideas that people tell them that they are unable to verify, even if the person is an authority, but they should use their reason. In his medical book *Aphorisms,* he wrote:

> If anyone tells you that he has proof from his personal experience of something that he needs to confirm his theory, even though he is recognized as a man of great authority and truthfulness – sincere and

moral – yet because he is so anxious for you to believe his notion, do not hesitate. Do not allow yourself to be swayed by the novelties that he tells you. Examine his theory and belief carefully…. Look into the matter. Don't let yourself be persuaded.

Summary

The story of Noah portrays a man who accepted what he was told without thought or comment. He was a man of faith who fulfilled the divine command without question. Could he have saved lives by acting differently? We will never know. But it seems clear that he should have tried. He was unlike Abraham and virtually all other biblical figures that constantly used their intellect and raised questions. We ask: "Can an unreasoning person of faith, who does nothing more than follow what he is told, be considered righteous?" The ancient sages agree that he did not act properly; however, they differed on whether his unreasoning behavior was righteous or whether he was a righteous fool.

*   *   *

In the affairs of this world, men are not saved by faith, but by avoiding and surpassing it.
> –Benjamin Franklin, Poor Richard's Almanac

The Synagogue officials were united. Even the rabbi agreed. They had all seen that the poor man was suffering. So they gathered at the east wing of the Synagogue and prayed in unison, "Please God, please allow the poor man to win the lottery so that he can eat!" When Wednesday came and his name was not announced, the group gathered again at the east wing. Again they prayed, full of faith, "Please God, please let this poor man win the lottery so that he can eat!" When Wednesday came and they saw the same result, they prayed again. After the third failure, the rabbi addressed God, "Why Lord, why didn't he win?" A voice came from heaven, "He never bought a ticket."

Lekh Lekha

Are some Midrashim based on Greek Philosophy?

Some people know the imaginative midrashic anecdotes about biblical characters more than they know what the Bible itself states. Thus, for example, when a poll was taken of a large group of people asking if the story of Abraham secretly breaking his father's idols is in the Bible, many swore that it is. They are surprised to hear that it is not. Midrashim have value, but must be used properly.

Questions
1. What is Midrash?
2. Should Jews accept midrashic stories as true history?
3. What is the source of midrashic stories and elaborations?

What is Midrash?
Midrash is a series of books written at various times by numerous authors with diverse agendas and different titles, containing Jewish interpretation and elaborations of Scripture. Generally, the Midrashim, the plural of Midrash, are arranged in the form of commentaries or sermons on various books of the Bible.

Midrashim have many forms. One is the imaginative elaboration of the Scriptural text. These Midrashim state that things occurred that are not mentioned, or in some cases not even hinted, in the Bible. An example is the story of Abraham crushing his father's idols, mentioned above. Scripture does not even hint at this story. Another example is the Midrash based on *Genesis* 22, where the Bible does not record what happened between the times that Abraham left his home with his son Isaac and two attendants to sacrifice his son and three days later, when they approached their destination. Various Midrashim fill the gap with different imaginative episodes that are not suggested by the text.

We do not know when the Midrashim were first composed. Some believe that they existed as early as the days of Moses and were passed on orally from one generation to another. Others suppose that they were composed later, at various periods, as Bible readers began to ask questions about the text.

Should Jews accept midrashic stories as true history?

In the introduction that he wrote to the Talmud, Samuel HaNagid (993–1055/6) wrote that Jews are not obligated to accept as true any midrashic statement, story, wisdom or ethics that were simply composed to narrate a story or relate a moral lesson, or even if it was written to explain Scripture, if it does not express *halakhah,* Jewish law.

Moses Maimonides (1138–1204) had another view. In his introduction to the *Mishnah Chelek,* in *Sanhedrin,* he states that those who take the midrashic stories literally are fools, so too are those who dismiss them out of hand, for the proper approach is to seek the meaning that the sages are imparting. Midrashim have wisdom, but they must be mined for better understanding.

What is the source of the Midrashim?

We do not know the source of the Midrashim. The story of Abraham crushing his father's idols, for example, was probably drawn from the almost identical episode in *Judges* 6, where the judge Gideon is described as secretly crushing his father's idols and later, like Abraham, rising to become a leader of his people.

It is interesting to note that some Midrashim are found in the writings of non-Jews, such as the Greek non-Jewish mystical and religiously-minded philosopher Plato (427 – 347 B.C.E.). Plato's tales, like the Midrashim, were also written to teach lessons – as he himself claims – and like them, require much thought to garner their meaning. In his *Laws,* Plato calls his myths "useful fiction (composed for) persuading all men to act justly in all things willingly and without constraint."

In the year 385 B.C.E., Plato composed his dramatic dialogue *Symposium,* the dinner party. While the primary focus of the party's discussion was Socrates' definition of "love," the treatise also contains a myth that is also related, with some variations, in Jewish Midrashim.

The year 385 was a time in Jewish history about which little is known. The Jews were living for the most part either in Judea or Babylon. They were under the control of the Persians. The Persians had contacts with the Greeks. The *Symposium* itself discusses some Persian traits. There had been wars between Greece and Persia shortly before this date. In this same period the Persians had also used Greek mercenaries in their wars.

There is evidence that some Greeks, including Plato, traveled in Syria, Egypt and Phoenicia, lands that bordered Judea, and many talked and shared ideas with the inhabitants of these lands. Thus, there was probably some contact between Jews and Greeks, including Plato, in the early fourth century.

There is no way of knowing the source of Plato's "myths." He could have taken them from early Jewish Midrashim or from men or women that he met during these contacts. Alternatively, Jews may have heard the stories from Plato or read them in his books. They may have inserted them in their Midrashim after seeing that they were, in their opinion, suggested by the biblical text.

Examples of Greek myths in the Midrashim

One Platonic myth in the *Symposium* is the story of the origin of the division of males and females. The story is told in the volume by the comic dramatist Aristophanes. According to Aristophanes, as reported by Plato, men and women were originally created as a single being, with four hands and legs and two faces. They were bisected by the god Zeus as punishment for their pride when they attempted to ascend to heaven and conquer the god. "Love," according to this myth, is the desire, need or attempt by people to regain their former happy state by reuniting with their lost half.

The *Midrash Genesis Rabbah* 8:1, the Babylonian Talmud *Berachot* 61a, *Eruvin* 18a and other sources relate the story of Adam being created as an androgynous being. While Plato retold the myth to explain the attraction of love, the Midrash and Talmud used it to explain why *Genesis* 1:27 reports that "male and female created He [God] them," while 2:21 states that Eve was made from Adam's rib. This parable, one of many explanations offered by the rabbis to explain the texts, states that originally Adam and Eve were a single being, but Eve was later separated from Adam.

Another example of a midrashic story appearing in Plato is Plato's myth in his *Republic* of the soul being taught knowledge before its birth, but then, just prior to birth, it is made to forget. Plato uses the story to stress the concept of the immortality of the soul (that the soul existed before it came to reside in our bodies), the idea of transmigration of souls (that it passes from one body to another after death) and how humans learn. According to Plato, learning is in essence remembering what one had learned before birth. Teaching, then, is stimulating a person to remember what he knew before he was born.

The *Midrash Tanchuma Pekude* 3 has a very similar story. Prior to birth, an angel teaches a soul all that it should know. The angel then places the soul in the womb of its future mother where it resides, still remembering what it had learned, for nine months. At the conclusion of this period, when the child is about to be born, the angel taps the child (above the mouth) causing the child to forget all that the soul had learned. The child enters the world crying for his or her loss of shelter, security, and knowledge.

Some explain that the midrashic version highlights the wonderful nature of the heavenly world. It is suggesting that if the soul would recall its existence in heaven and all that it knew before birth, it would be reluctant to partake of anything in this world. Yet, the soul retains some sense, an almost unconscious sense, of what it had learned and humans must do all they can to get (back) in touch with this sense of the divine.

Still another example is the statement that Plato made in his *Laws*. He writes that in the beginning of the world "reason set in order all that is in heaven." He also states that man "must be able to give a rational explanation of all that admits of rational explanation." This concept that the world was created by and functions with wisdom is in many Jewish sources. The Aramaic translation of the Bible called *Neophyti*, for instance, renders the opening verse of *Genesis* "With wisdom God created the heaven and the earth."

Summary

Midrashim are commentaries on the Bible that may appear to have fanciful, even illogical elements, but which were written to convey moral and theological lessons to the Jewish people. One may have to pay close attention to the Midrash to derive the lesson. Some of the stories in the Midrashim are also in non-Jewish sources, including Greek myths. It is often impossible to know which appeared first, the myth or the Midrash. The Jewish philosopher Philo, who lived in Alexandria at the beginning of the Common Era, wrote in his

Questions and Solutions in Genesis 3:5 that the Greeks were "snatching" many of their ideas from Moses and the Torah "like thieves." However, he may be incorrect. It is possible, though far-fetched, that both cultures developed the same tales independently, but used them differently. It may also be that an early version of the Midrash is the source for the Greek myth, and the Greeks fit the story's moral to its concept of the world. It is also likely that rabbis retold some Greek legends in their Midrashim and Talmuds, after revising them to fit their Jewish ideology.

Vayeira

How does God speak? Rabbi Akiva vs. Rabbi Ishmael

The question "How does God speak to us in the Bible" is very complicated and is the subject of many disputes. The most important opinions on the subject are those of Rabbi Akiva and Rabbi Ishmael, both of whom died in the early part of the second century.

Questions
1. What are the two major ancient differences in interpreting the Bible?
2. Why did the two scholars who presented the two interpretations hold their views?

Rabbi Akiva and Rabbi Ishmael
Rabbi Akiva and Rabbi Ishmael lived during the first third of the second century C.E. Rabbi Akiva was convinced that since the Torah emanated from God, it must address humans with a divine voice. Since God is all wise, he felt that it is inconceivable that God would utter a single word, or even a single letter, unless He was communicating something of importance. Therefore, he concluded, there is no extra word in Scripture; indeed, every word, even every letter, was written by an omniscient deity and has a distinct divine message.

While his colleague focused on the celestial origin of the Torah, Rabbi Ishmael concentrated on the recipient. People are not godly and can not be expected to understand heavenly language. The Torah was written for humans not for God and not for angels. Thus it must be communicated in a fashion that humans can understand. Rabbi Ishmael's famous statement is *dibra torah k'lashon b'nei adam*, "the Torah speaks in the language of man." Thus, just as man repeats himself, occasionally exaggerates to make a point, adds language simply to beautify sentences, so, too, does the Torah.

A somewhat modern approach accepting the methodology of Rabbi Ishmael

In 1753, the biblical scholar Robert Lowth wrote about what is now considered the modern view of "parallelisms," the frequent appearance in the Bible of parallel statements. He gives many examples of the parallels and systematizes them into different categories. However, like Rabbi Ishmael, he notes that parallels are used to make statements in a beautiful and readable manner.

The prevailing view

The outlook of Rabbi Akiva has, for unknown reasons, become the preferred approach used in understanding Scripture. Thus, when the Bible reiterates its thought, as it frequently does, the rabbis will ask, what message is the repetition teaching us?

Examples
Rashi

This interpretive methodology is prevalent in Rashi (1040–1105), the most popular of Bible commentators. His treatment of *Genesis* 21:1 is a good example. The text reads, "The Lord remembered Sarah as He had said, and the Lord did to Sarah as He had spoken." Rabbi Ishmael would no doubt say that the Bible is recapping a single thought in a poetic fashion. God "remembered" and "did" – both portray that God kept His pledge to give Sarah a son. Similarly, both "said" and "spoken" refer to this same promise.

However, Rashi followed the technique of Rabbi Akiva and wrote that the passage is referring to two separate incidents. "Remembered" means that God made Sarah pregnant and "did" that he gave her a son. Nachmanides (1195–1270), who also generally follows the Akivian system, but does not do so here, points out correctly that "remembered" is never used in the Bible for pregnancy and that it means birth, just as "did." However, Rashi is bothered by the repetition, which like Rabbi Akiva he felt must be saying something different than the first utterance.

Pseudo-Jonathan

The Aramaic translation of the Bible known as *Pseudo-Jonathan* (generally dated in the ninth or tenth century) renders this verse with an eye to Rabbi Akiva. It turns the text into two separate instances and recasts them to refer to Abraham rather than Sarah. It records that: "The Lord remembered Sarah as He had said to him [meaning, that God's response was his promise to Abraham, not Sarah, in *Genesis* 18:14]. And [in addition, He] performed a sign for Sarah [she had a son]. [The son came as a result of prayer] like the time that Abraham prayed on Abimelech's behalf [that Abimelech be cured and be able to have children]."

Looking at the plain meaning of the text

Rabbi Ishmael not only interprets the Bible as if it were speaking in human language, but he stresses that we must look at the plain or simple meaning of the text and not read imaginative notions into the verse that are not in its plain meaning. The rational interpreters of the Bible follow this practice. Let's look at some examples.

The Decalogue

Probably the most famous instance of repetitions is the dual versions of the Decalogue, named the Ten Statements *(Eser HaDibrot)* in Hebrew, but commonly called the Ten Commandments in English, even though the Ten Statements have more than ten commands. There is one version of it in *Exodus* 20 and a repetition in *Deuteronomy* 5. The two are dissimilar in many ways, including altered wording, the addition of explanations in *Deuteronomy*, and the changed spellings of some words. Those who follow the Akivian method insist that the variations were intentionally made to teach lessons not in the first iteration. Thus, focusing on the wordings of the Sabbath command, *zachor* in *Exodus* and *shamor* in *Deuteronomy*, usually translated "remember" and "keep," respectively, Rashi, Nachmanides, Midrashim and Talmuds give various reasons for the alteration, saying that each is teaching a distinct lesson. In contrast, ibn Ezra (1089–1164) points out that the two words are simply two ways of saying the same thing. He explains that *Exodus* contains the divine version of the Decalogue and *Deuteronomy* is Moses' explanation of it.

Deuteronomy 33:10

Deuteronomy 33:10 is another example. The Bible states "let them teach your statutes to Jacob, your teachings to Israel." The *Midrash Sifre* follows the Akivian system when it turns a blind eye to the parallelisms and states that "statutes" means the written Torah and "teachings" the oral law. This is clever *derash* (explanation), but a plain reading of the text, here and elsewhere in Scripture, reveals no overt mention of an oral law.

Genesis 24:1

Another instance is *Genesis* 24:1. It has a dual statement, "Abraham was old, advanced in age." The *Midrash Genesis Rabbah*, famous for narrative elaborations of the scriptural text, finds two things. Some people are blessed with dignity in old age without having a lengthy life, while others have a long life without dignity. Abraham had both. Again, this is a clever interpretation and an important teaching, but there is no hint of "dignity" in the plain reading of the passage.

Genesis 22:12

A final example of a multitude that can be cited is *Genesis* 22:12. Abraham is stopped from sacrificing his son Isaac when he envisions an angel telling him in parallel form, "Do not harm the boy, do nothing to him." The *Midrash Genesis Rabbah* explains the two statements as a response to two incidences. The angel told Abraham to cease. This is the first statement. Abraham pleaded: I will stop, but let me just take a drop of blood from my son. This will be a token that shows that I did what God commanded. At this point, the angel stresses: "do nothing to him." The midrashic imaginative conversation is not suggested by the text itself and is indeed inconsistent with what we are told of Abraham: he was willing to sacrifice his son since he understood that God commanded it. But he would never have offered to kill or maim or even hurt his beloved son on his own.

Summary

Realizing that there are these two methods of explaining the text, one should ask, as he or she hears an interpretation: Is this the plain meaning of the text? Am I being told something that the text does not even suggest? Was the interpretation developed because the commentator refused to view the Bible as simply making a beautiful parallel statement?

Chayei Sarah

Did Sarah act improperly?

Several related incidences in the life and death of Abraham and Sarah raise questions:

Questions
1. Did Sarah and Abraham act improperly?
2. Are the episodes in the life of the senior patriarchs interpreted differently by some Bible commentators, although they looked at the same facts?
3. Can the interpretation by a commentator based upon the rendering of a translator be incorrect?
4. Can a commentator propose two opposite interpretations of what transpired?

Three texts
Genesis 23:1 is literally translated, "The life of Sarah was a hundred years, twenty years and seven years; [these were] the years of Sarah's life." Rashi (1040–1105) comments upon the three-fold repetition of "years": "This tells us that each phrase should be interpreted as a separate fact. At the age of one hundred, she was like twenty in respect to sin, for a twenty year old is not considered a sinner since she is not liable for [divine] punishment; so at one hundred, she was without sin." Rashi's source was the *Midrash Genesis Rabbah* 58:1.

Is it correct to say that Sarah did not sin? Doesn't everybody know that she sinned when she laughed when she was told that she would have a child in her old age? This phrase "everybody knows" is interesting; whenever you hear it you know that in many instances what will follow will probably be wrong. What is the truth about this matter?

As with many things connected with the Bible, commentators disagree whether or not Sarah acted improperly. The sources that need to be examined are *Genesis* 17 and 18.

In *Genesis* 17:16 and 17, God appears to Abraham and assures him, "I will give you a son from her [Sarah]…. Then Abraham fell upon his face *vayitchak* (and he laughed). He said in his heart, 'Can a child be born to a person who is a hundred years old'" Abraham apparently did not relate this promise to his wife.

In *Genesis* 18, Abraham is visited by three strangers, who are identified as angels after they left. He feeds them while his wife Sarah remained behind the tent entrance, apparently complying with the custom of the time. However, she overheard their conversation. One of the strangers remarkably assures Abraham in verses 10 to 12, "Sarah your wife will have a son. Sarah hears from the door of the tent, which was behind him…. And Sarah laughed [the Hebrew is the feminine form of the same word used to describe Abraham's reaction *vatizchak*] within herself saying, 'Can I have [this] pleasure after I have become old and my lord is old?'"

Interpretations of the texts

The reaction of both Abraham and Sarah seems to be identical. Both laugh. The same Hebrew word for laughter is used for both, except, as required by Hebrew grammar, the feminine form is used for Sarah and the masculine for her husband. Both laugh inwardly. The only difference is that Abraham is described as laughing *b'libo*, "in his heart," and Sarah *b'kirbah*, "within herself." The two words seem to be synonyms. Were their reactions the same? Did one react reprehensibly? Were they both shady?

Nachmanides (1195–1270) thought that Sarah, and certainly Abraham, behaved as befitted a patriarch and matriarch. He saw that Sarah responded with derision, but felt it was proper. Sarah, he felt, simply did not believe the strangers. She did not know that they were angels. She probably did not see them. Thus, it was reasonable that she relied on what she considered to be normal, that women do not give birth at age ninety. Radak and Sforno agreed with this interpretation. The latter wrote, "She thought that the words of the angel were only the blessing from some prophet," and not a promise from God.

The *Midrash Genesis Rabbah* took the opposite position. It understood that Sarah acted inappropriately. The Midrash relates that when the Jews of Alexandria translated the Pentateuch into Greek, and produced the work known as the Septuagint, they altered the text so that the non-Jews who read it would be able to understand why God was dissatisfied with Sarah's behavior. They rendered (Sarah laughed) *b'kirbah*, "within herself," as if it stated *b'k'rovah*, "among her relatives." The new reading, as Rashi explains in the Babylonian Talmud (*Megillah* 9a), makes it clear to the Greek readers that God was displeased because Sarah made a public display of her laughter, whereas Abraham laughed only within himself.

Contradictory interpretations

Rashi to 23:1, as we mentioned above, stated that Sarah did not sin. However, in his commentary to 17:17, in a remark that seems to be inconsistent with his 23:1 opinion, he notes that the Aramaic translation of the Pentateuch known as *Targum Onkelos* (composed around the year 400 C.E.) paraphrases the verb *vayitzchak*, "and he laughed," regarding Abraham as "and he rejoiced." *Onkelos* did not paraphrase Sarah's *vatitzchak*, "and she laughed." "This," writes Rashi, "teaches that Abraham believed [God's promise] and rejoiced, but Sarah did not believe it and sneered. Therefore the Holy One, blessed be He, was angry with Sarah, but He was not angry with Abraham."

How can we explain what appears to be an instance where Rashi is contradicting himself? It is possible that Rashi indeed felt that Sarah did not act improperly, as indicated in 23:1, while his comment on 17:17 was not his own idea, but rather an expansion of *Onkelos*.

Did Rashi understand *Onkelos*?

It is possible that *Onkelos* may not have intended to disparage Sarah, as Rashi understands the Aramaic text. The targumist may have changed the word for Abraham to clarify that he was not acting unfittingly. He may have felt that Sarah also acted correctly, but could not change her "laughed" to "rejoiced," since 18:13 reports, "the Lord asked Abraham, 'Why did Sarah laugh?'" If the targumist would have said she "rejoiced," God's question would have been meaningless. Therefore, feeling that he was unable to rewrite the later text, he could not change "laughed."

However, it should, in all fairness be noted that the Aramaic translations of *Pseudo-Jonathan* and *Neophyti* alter 18:12 to indicate that Sarah "wondered," instead of "laughed," and they retain God's question, "Why did Sarah laugh?"

They were not worried about this matter. Thus, it is likely that Rashi was correct in his interpretation of this *Onkelos* translation.

Alternative interpretations

Joseph Bechor Shor (born around 1080), who was a student of Rashi's grandson Rabbeinu Tam, gives alternative interpretations of the two incidences of the revelation of the future birth of Isaac. In his comment on 17:17, he writes that Abraham's act of falling on his face shows that he believed that God was performing a miracle for him, and he was expressing thanks. However, in his remarks on 17:19, he offers the alternative idea that both Abraham and Sarah acted unacceptably when they heard God assure them of the birth of a son, and God in a discrete manner criticized both of them indirectly. He did not tell Sarah that she was wrong, but instructed Abraham to do so. Because a person can accept criticism better if they get it indirectly. God also did not criticize Abraham openly. He told him to call his son Isaac, in Hebrew *Yitzchak*, meaning "laughter." This, states Bechor Shor, was a broad hint that Abraham should not have laughed.

Summary

Thus we see that the commentators disagree on whether Sarah and Abraham acted correctly. Some say they both did. Others, that Sarah did not. Still others, that both were wrong. We saw also that Rashi may have contradicted himself on the subject and that Bechor Shor offered alternative views.

Toldot

Obscurities in Scripture

The biblical portion of *Toldot* relates that Isaac married Rebecca when he was forty years of age, but, like the matriarchs Sarah before her and Rachel afterwards, his wife was barren. Isaac entreated God for her and she conceived twins who struggled in her womb.

Understandably in pain, confused and distraught, she exclaimed in 25:22, *im kein lama zeh anochi*, and went out and petitioned God to explain what was happening to her. God responded by telling her that she had two sons in her womb who would develop into separate nations.

Questions
1. What does *im kein lama zeh anochi* mean?
2. Why are there obscurities and ambiguities in the Bible?

Rebecca's obscure reaction
The Hebrew words in the above quote describing Rebecca's reaction are obscure and have been translated and explained in various ways. The words literally mean, when translated in the order of the original Hebrew, "If so, why this I?" or out of order and with the addition of clearly implied words, but still literally, "If [this is] so [that I am in such pain], why [am] I this?" What is "this?" Is she making a question or a statement? More important, what is Rebecca talking about?

The problem is that the sentence lacks a predicate. The "lack" is what is known as an ellipsis. In English, an ellipsis is frequently shown by dots, such as this…. It is important to know that there are many ellipses, the plural form of the word, in Scripture. An ellipsis is a grammatical description of a sentence where one or more words that are needed to complete a sentence in a clear fashion is missing. It is a broken-off sentence. What is missing in Rebecca's wail is the direct object. What is Rebecca crying about?

Obscurities in the Bible

Anyone who tries to understand the Bible should know that ellipses exist. Unfortunately, many of us read the Bible only in a translation. The translators remove the obscurity with their understanding of what was meant. For example, in this verse, The Jewish Publication Society's *Holy Scripture* of 1917 and 1955 translates, "If it be so, wherefore do I live?" Their *The Torah* of 1962 has "If so, why do I exist?" Robert Alter, in his 1996 *Genesis,* renders it "Then why me?"

The absence of words obviously creates an obscurity or ambiguity. This fact does not mean that the Torah text is corrupt. All good literature contains obscurities and ambiguities. This leaves the readers an opportunity to interpret the incident as they will. This is what the Argentinean novelist Jorge Borges (born 1899) meant when he said that two people write good literature, the writer and the reader. One can also understand the value of an obscurity by thinking of a painting. The artist may have meant one thing when he painted the object, but we can read into it what we see and feel is appropriate. Rebecca's lament is an example of this phenomenon.

Various interpretations

The following different interpretations dramatize some of the various approaches taken to decipher the obscurity in this verse.

The ancient Syriac translation of the Bible named the *Peshitta,* the Aramaic translation called the *Fragmented Targum* (the dates of these documents are widely debated by scholars), and Nachmanides (1195–1270) add words to clarify the verse as: "Why do I live?"

The *Midrash Genesis Rabbah* 63:6 (edited in the early fifth century C.E.), the Aramaic translations of *Pseudo-Jonathan* (about the ninth century) and *Neophyti* (of a debated date), and Rashi (1040–1105) paraphrase it as, "If so, why would I want to have children?"

The Arabic translation of Saadiah Gaon (882–942) has, "If I would have known that matters would turn out as they did, I would have never requested [to have children]."

Sforno (born about 1470) has her think about the past and wander, "Why did my husband and my family insist that I be the mother of Isaac's children?"

Ibn Ezra (1089–1164) and Radak (about 1160–1235) have Rebecca ask, like the child at the Passover Seder, "Why is my pregnancy different than all other pregnancies?"

Chizkunee (about the eleventh century) pictures her in such distress that she laments, "Why should I live and bear so much pain? It would have been better if I died and had no pain!"

Joseph Bechor Shor (born about 1080) sees her as being unable to understand how God functions, "Why did God grant my prayer since what He did does not help me?" Not all translators or commentators explained the ellipsis.

The fact that there are such different interpretations highlights that there are obscurities in the Bible. These obscurities enhance the literary value of and interest in the story. Different people, including experts in the field, offer different ideas as to what Scripture intended. Thus, anyone who insists that he or she "knows" what was meant should be listened to with incredulity.

*   *   *

Another obscurity

This obscurity is not the only one in this narrative. The sages note that virtually all the matriarchs were barren for many years (Leah was an exception) but the Bible does not explain why this happened. The sages ask why, and give many different explanations.

*   *   *

Another ellipses and obscurity

In view of the significance and frequency of ellipses, it is worth looking at another one. *Genesis* 4:8 states, "Cain said to his brother Abel…and it was when they were in the field, Cain rose against Abel his brother and killed him." What Cain said to Abel is missing. Robert Alter, in his *Genesis* notes the ellipsis and adds the statement that was inserted in the Greek Septuagint (250 B.C.E.), the Syriac Peshitta translation (early part of the first millennium C.E.), the *Targums Pseudo-Jonathan* and *Neophyti*, and Nachmanides, "Let us go out to the field."

Some commentators and translators read the text as if it sated, "Cain came to Abel with words."

Rashi states that Cain came with words of complaint, words that justified him killing his brother.

Ibn Ezra feels that the words were his report of what God had told him about his sacrifice.

Radak adds that he blamed his brother for God's reaction.

We should also note that the verse has another obscurity, although it is not an ellipsis; it does not explain why Cain "rose against Abel and killed him." The treatment of the ellipsis by Alter does not clarify this obscurity. However, Rashi, ibn Ezra and Radak elaborate upon the ellipsis with an eye to explaining the obscurity. They inform us what Cain said (the ellipsis) and why he felt he wanted to kill his brother (the obscurity).

We should also note that ellipses and obscurities frequently lead to imaginative midrashic elaborations of the biblical narrative. On this verse, the *Midrash Genesis Rabbah* 12:7 states:

> What did they fight about? They said, "Come and let us divide the world." One then took the land and the other that which is movable. The first then said, "The land you are standing on is mine." The other retorted, "You are wearing what belongs to me." One then said, "strip!" The other retorted, "Fly [off the ground]!" A quarrel followed and Cain rose up against his brother.

The Midrash has another interpretation: they divided the land and movables equally but squabbled about on whose lands the future Israelite Temple would be built. The Aramaic *Targums Pseudo-Jonathan* and *Neophyti* have still another interpretation. The brothers disputed about how the world functions and whether "mercy" impacts upon its functioning. Needless to say, there are also other opinions about their disagreement.

Summary

The Bible is filled with obscure verses. These gave the ancient commentators and translators opportunities to interpret the text according to traditions they received or as they saw fit. This also gives us a chance to participate, to form our own notions of what happened and create our own understanding of the scriptural story.

Vayeitzei

Do Jews believe in angels?

The Bible and prayers mention angels, but Jews differed in the past and still do today on the existence of angels. Should we interpret these allusions symbolically, and deny the existence of angels? Or, should we take these references literally, and insist that not only do angels exist but that they are involved in and impact upon our lives?

Questions
1. Do angels exist?
2. If not, how should we understand the statements about angels in Jewish literature, including the prayer book, the Siddur?

Angels visiting Jewish homes on Friday night
The popular and melodious Friday evening song Shalom Alechem is an example. Sung jointly by the family, it unambiguously welcomes angels into the Jewish home on the Sabbath. According to tradition, two angels join the worshipper and accompany him from the Synagogue on Friday evening. One angel wants to do good and the other is bent on mischief. If, upon reaching the home, the first sees that the home has been prepared in an exemplary fashion for the Sabbath, with warm lights and delicious food, the family dressed in their finest, the wine bottle next to a lovely kiddush cup, the braided challah covered by a decorative cloth, he blesses the home, "may it be so next week." If the home is ill prepared, if little or no attention has been given to the Sabbath, the other angel expresses his choice that it continue in disarray. Rational Jews understand the story as a symbolic lesson to organize our lives suitably for the Sabbath. They know that proper preparation will aid in assuring future delights. The non-rationalist accepts the tale literally, and anxiously hopes that the bad angel will not harm him and his family.

Jacob and angels

In *Genesis* 28:12 one can find one of many instances of biblical references to angels. Jacob abandoned his family home fearing the revenge of his brother Esau for taking the blessing his father Isaac intended for him. He has a dream on the first night away from home in which his fear is expressed. He sees a ladder reaching as far as heaven with angels ascending and descending its steps. The episode is easy for rationalists to understand. The Bible is stating that the angels were symbolic figures in his dream, not actual beings. It is obvious to rationalists that Jacob understands that the angels are assurances of his security and his fear is assuaged. The non-rationalist sees the dream as biblical confirmation of his belief in the existence of angels.

What is an angel?

The term *malakh*, which is frequently translated "angel," literally means "messenger." The rationalist understands the term as a metaphor for the acts of God and the forces of nature. The non-rationalist, on the other hand, is convinced that it is a noun describing a supernatural being that is superior to humans in power and knowledge, but not as powerful as God. Some non-rationalists also believe in the existence of incorporeal life forms that perform evil act, frequently contrary to God's will. They may name them demons or evil angels.

Maimonides

Moses Maimonides (1138–1204) and Moses Nachmanides (1195–1270) express polar opposite beliefs regarding angels, although there are many other intermediate ideas. Maimonides totally rejected the literal notion that angels are divine-like almost human-like beings that perform missions for God. Maimonides was certain that it is inconceivable that God would need help from independent forces. God created the laws of nature that accomplished all that He wanted, all that was needed, and all that was good. Furthermore, it is impossible to understand how such divine-like body-less spirits could be seen by man. Just as God lacks any body form, and therefore could not be seen, so, too, angels, who are said to be incorporeal, would be unseeable.

Maimonides discusses angels in his *Guide of the Perplexed* 2:6. He states there that angels certainly exist, after all the Bible mentions them, but the word should be understood figuratively. An angel is the various forces of the laws of nature: "every act of God is described as being performed by an angel." The word "angel means messenger; hence everything that is given a certain mission is an angel." The book of *Psalms* 104:4 makes it clear that even the "elements are called angels, 'who makes winds, His angels.'"

Maimonides explains that when Scripture mentions that someone saw an angel, it simply means that he had a dream or vision. In short, Maimonides maintains that his view is identical "with the opinion of [the Greek philosopher] Aristotle. There is only a difference in the names employed." Aristotle taught that the world functions according to the laws of nature and so did Maimonides.

Nachmanides

Nachmanides disagreed entirely. He was convinced that the world does not function according to the laws of nature. God is directly and daily involved in every occurrence on earth, even the most mundane, such as a leaf falling from a tree.

He frequently discusses the ramifications of his belief in his Bible commentaries, in *Genesis* 17:1 and 46:15, *Exodus* 13:16, *Leviticus* 26:11, and other places. Thus, for example, only God and not doctors can heal people (*Exodus* 21:19).

Nachmanides argued that people can see angels. This happened in *Genesis* 16:11 when Hagar, Abraham's concubine, saw an angel. It occurred also to Abraham when he saw three of them in *Genesis* 18:2. Jacob wrestled with one in *Genesis* 32:25. Balaam encountered one in *Numbers* 22:31. Isaac was saved by one who appeared to his father Abraham in *Genesis* 22:11. These are just a few of many examples cited by Nachmanides.

He was also convinced that demons exist and that they interact with people. Since they can harm people, he outlined a method to avoid their harm in *Leviticus* 16:7.

Zohar

Nachmanides view also appears in such mystical works as the *Zohar*. The *Zohar* pictures Abraham accompanying the angels for part of their journey when they left him. "But, if Abraham knew they were angels," asks the *Zohar*, "why did he accompany them? Because he treated them like human beings."

Summary
Needless to say, one may believe as one chooses. Virtually any idea that one has about angels can find support in the view of some ancient sage. However, one should remember that ideas can have a significant impact upon human lives. They can encourage people to develop intellectually and motivate them to act properly. Alternatively, a wrong belief can give people the assurance that they are surrounded by protective supernatural forces. Such a notion stifles their thinking and induces them to be passive and indifferent, vegetating, instead of living in this world and contributing to mankind.

What prompted Jacob to wrestle an angel?

The extraordinary and astonishing episode of Jacob wrestling an angel at the Wadi Jabbok raises many questions and an assortment of conflicting answers, including the following:

Questions

1. Assuming that angels exist and that Jacob started the fight, what prompted him to fight an angel?
2. Is it at all possible to wrestle an angel?
3. Who in their right mind would expect to wrestle an angel and be victorious?
4. If the angel started the fight, could we imagine that God would allow an angel to defeat a righteous patriarch?
5. Why did the fight happen at the Wadi Jabbok?
6. What is the significance of Jacob being called Israel after he bested the angel?
7. What is the implication of Jacob being wounded on his hip?
8. Why did the Israelites commemorate the episode by abstaining from eating the thigh-vein?

The text

The wrestling episode is related in *Genesis* 32:25–33. Jacob had reached the Wadi Jabbok on his return home after an absence from Canaan of some twenty years. He was about to face his brother Esau who had wanted to kill him twenty years earlier as revenge for Jacob taking the blessing that their father Isaac intended to give to Esau. During the night, Jacob took his family across the Wadi Jabbok and entered Canaan. Then he returned to the other side where he was alone.

While there, "a man wrestled with him until the break of day. [The man is called *Elohim* in verses 29 and 31, suggesting that he was an angel.] When he [the man] saw that he could not beat him, he touched the hollow of his thigh;

and the hollow of the thigh was uprooted as he wrestled with him." The man begged Jacob to let him go. Jacob agreed if he would bless him. The man asked his name. He answered "Jacob." The man said his name will no longer be Jacob but Israel, "for you wrestled with God and with men and prevailed." He blessed Jacob. In the morning, Jacob was limping. "Therefore the Israelites do not eat the thigh-vein... because he touched Jacob's thigh-vein."

Conflicting interpretations
Maimonides

The commentators disagree in interpreting the episode. The rationalist Maimonides (1138–1204) insisted that angels do not exist; they are metaphors for the natural forces of the divine. In his *Guide of the Perplexed* 2:42, he explains that Jacob never wrestled an angel; this was a vision.

While he does not explain the episode in detail, David Kimchi (1160–1235) and Joseph ibn Kaspi (born around 1280) do so, using Maimonides' basic assumptions.

Jacob returned to Canaan after his long absence, frightened and agitated over his upcoming confrontation with his brother Esau, from whom he had fled twenty years earlier, fearing for his life. He carried his family across the Wadi Jabbok, the boundary into Canaan, crossing "his Rubicon," and he returned to the other side for some moments of contemplation.

With the upcoming confrontation in his mind, he fell asleep; and nervously dreamed of a symbolic struggle with his brother. He tussled and fought, but felt victorious in his dream. He awoke, as most people do even after a successful battle, with some minor injury. He rose from his bed with some assurance about his future meeting with his brother.

Jacob's descendants remembered their ancestor's struggle by abstaining from eating the thigh-vein. The memory gives them the strength and confidence to face and overcome their own difficulties.

Abravanel

The Spanish Bible commentator Don Isaac Abravanel (1437–1508) asked: if this was only a dream as Maimonides contends, how come Jacob awoke limping? He answers with a keen understanding of psychology: some people dream so realistically that they feel the consequences of the dream when they awake.

Targum Onkelos

The Aramaic translation of the Bible called *Targum Onkelos* (composed around the year 400 C.E.) substituted a word that denotes a verbal attempt to persuade, in place of "wrestled." The targumist reflects Maimonides' concept since he does not portray Jacob having anthropomorphic bodily contact with a celestial angel.

Bechor Shor and Rashbam

Joseph Bechor Shor and Rashbam were born around 1080. The first was a student of Rashi's grandson, Rabbeinu Tam, and the second was Rashi's grandson, the brother of Bechor Shor's teacher. Curiously, although they frequently interpret the text rationally, they seem to explain that Jacob actually wrestled with an angel.

Rashbam states that the angel was preventing Jacob from abandoning his resolution and fleeing Canaan because of his fear of Esau. By stopping the flight, God was able to fulfill His promise to Jacob that Esau would not harm him.

Jacob was hurt on his hip, according to these commentators, as a punishment for trying to avoid meeting Esau. Bechor Shor adds that the angel would have prevailed if God had not helped the patriarch.

Nachmanides and Rashi

We would have expected that Nachmanides (1195–1270) and Rashi (1040–1105) would describe a physical battle between Jacob and the angel. Remarkably, they fail to do so. They simply state what is contained in Scripture without any substantive elaboration. It is as if they are leaving it to the reader to decide whether they want to accept the story as it is literally presented. They may have realized that even if one believes in angels, it is totally irrational to suppose that one can wrestle with heavenly beings.

Midrash Genesis Rabbah

The *Midrash Genesis Rabbah* 77:4 (edited at the beginning of the fifth century C.E.), understands the story symbolically, but does not forbid us to believe it literally. The Midrash writes: "'He touched all the righteous people who were destined to come from Jacob.' Nachmanides interprets the Midrash to be referring to the persecutions of the Jews by the Romans before and after the battle of Bar Kochba in 132–135 C.E., who, like Jacob, will endure and ultimately have peace.

The Midrash also quotes the opinion of Rabbi Hama that the angel was the guardian of Esau. Needless to say, Maimonides would agree with Rabbi Hama, but would explain that Jacob had a dream encounter with Esau's symbolic guardian. Thus, it is unclear whether the Midrash understands the story literally.

Moses Alshich

In contrast to many others, the mystic Moses Alshich (1508– about 1600) describes Jacob wrestling with the angel with many imaginative details that are not in Scripture.

When Jacob brought his family across the Jabbok and later returned to its north non-Canaanite side alone, he lost, according to Alshich, the protection of the angels that were assigned protective duty in the land of Canaan. Until the crossing, angels of the diaspora accompanied Jacob and protected him. They left him when he crossed the Jabbok. When he made the crossing back to the northern side, the angels assigned the protective duty in Canaan, remained with his family on the southern side of the Jabbok.

God sent the "spiritual counterpart of Esau" to confront the unprotected Jacob because He wanted to show him that he did not need angelic assistance when he met Esau. God wanted him to battle the angel, defeat him, and realize that if he could beat an angel he could certainly prevail over his brother.

Alshich adds the thoughts of the angel in his commentary. The angel wondered how he could beat the patriarch. Then he remembered that Jacob had married two sisters, which was forbidden centuries later in the Torah. Jacob, Alshich believed, must have observed the Torah even before it was given to Moses, for he was a righteous man. Yet he violated this Torah law.

The angel understood this and saw sexuality as Jacob's weakness. Therefore the angel attacked his weakest point, his sexual organ.

Alshich claims that the Jews refrained afterwards from eating the thigh-vein, because this is symbolic of the male organ. The practice, according to him, reminds Jews not to be preoccupied with sex.

(This rather unusual interpretation was already attacked years before by the twelfth century rationalistic sage Abraham ibn Ezra [1089–1164]. Ibn Ezra noted in his commentary that some supposed that this body part was the focus of the attack. Ibn Ezra called the notion ridiculous.)

Alshich identifies the angel as Samael, one of the names of the devil. He explains that Samael did not want to tell Jacob who he was, because if Jacob knew he was the devil, Jacob would have hurt him badly.

Summary

Bible commentators disagree on whether Jacob physically wrestled an angel. Many are convinced that Scripture is describing a dream provoked by his understandable fear of his brother and his imminent contact with him. Others are ambiguous. However, Alshich made a clear statement that he accepted the narrative literally.

The commentators also quarrel why the Wadi Jabbok was the site of the struggle. The rationalists identify it as the border into Esau's territory, the area where Jacob expected to encounter his brother, the place that provoked his fear and the dream. Others see it as the secluded location where Jacob fled rather than face his brother. The angel appeared to halt his flight. Still another sees the boundary as the appropriate site where God could teach the patriarch that he could prevail over his brother.

Some posit that Jacob was struck on the hip simply to show that all struggles, even those that ultimately result in success, end with some wound. Others see it as a punishment for his attempted escape from Esau, even though God had promised that he would triumph. Another, somewhat fancifully, feels that it was a punishment for marrying two sisters.

Most agree that the Israelites refrain from eating the thigh-vein to remember the victory of their forefather and to be inspired that they will also prevail in their own travails. However, one rabbi, Alshich, contended that it reminds Jews to avoid preoccupation with sex.

All agree that Jacob was triumphant in his struggle and he was called Israel because of his success.

Vayeishev

May we enjoy life in this world?

One Midrash may disagree with another. One Midrash may report the view of a single individual or of a particular group, while another Midrash will express the idea of others. Some Midrashim may even go counter to our way of thinking. We will examine some of these Midrashim.

Questions
1. Should we try to enjoy life in this world?
2. What are some of the different views on the subject?
3. Why do bad things occur to good people?

The opinion of Rashi and a Midrash
Bad things happening to good people

Genesis 37 begins the story of Joseph and his brothers. The introductory sentence sets the stage, "Jacob dwelt in the land of his father's sojournings, in the land of Canaan."

The eleventh century French Bible commentator Rashi, who explained Scripture with Midrashim that he felt fit into the plain meaning of the text, explains this verse by paraphrasing the *Midrash Genesis Rabbah* (edited in the beginning of the fifth century C.E.). "Jacob wanted to dwell in peace, but the troubles of Joseph sprang upon him. The righteous want to dwell in peace, but the Holy One Blessed Be He said, 'Isn't what is prepared for them in the world-to-come enough for the righteous, but they want to dwell in peace [also] in this world!'"

The *Midrash* itself uses stronger and more figurative language, "When the righteous wish to dwell in tranquility in this world, Satan comes and accuses them: 'They are not content with what is in store for them in the hereafter, but they wish to dwell at ease even in this world!' The proof [that the righteous are acting improperly] lies in the fact that the patriarch Jacob wanted to live at ease in this world, whereupon he was attacked by Joseph's Satan."

The position of this *Midrash* is that bad things happen to good people in this world. The reward for good behavior is given in the world-to-come. It is even improper to expect to live in peace. Satan in the *Midrash* is a metaphor for natural troubles. The Midrash is insisting that Jacob made a mistake in thinking that he could settle in Canaan with a life of ease. As the saying goes, "Man thinks, but God laughs!"

What prompted this view?
This *Midrash* was compiled shortly after the Roman Emperor Constantine accepted Christianity as one of the allowable Roman religions. Many of the Christians of the fourth century used Constantine's "conversion" as an opportunity to make the life of Jews difficult. It is likely that a sizable number of Jews, including the authors of the opinion in this Midrash, recognized that they could not fight back They accepted the torment inflicted upon them, turned inward and sought peace outside of this world, in the hereafter. Is this the only attitude of Judaism? No! There are those that disagree. They feel that this is not the proper Jewish view and that it is an unhealthy approach.

Enjoying things in this world
Rashi himself presents the opposite view on whether one can enjoy what is in this world. He paraphrases the fourth century *Midrash Sifre* on *Numbers* 6:11, where a sage states the opposite of what is in *Genesis Rabbah*.

Rashi writes about the Nazir (Nazirite), a person who vowed that he would not drink wine and abstain from other things for a certain period. The Bible states that the Nazir must bring a sin offering at the end of the period of the vow. Rashi mentions one opinion that he must bring the sin offering "because he afflicted himself [by abstaining] from wine."

The corresponding *Midrash* itself is more expansive, "Now if he who afflicted himself [by abstaining] from wine must bring a sin offering, how much more would we expect one [to require atonement if he restricts himself] from everything." The sage who stated what we quoted obviously disagrees with the view we cited earlier about Jacob from the *Midrash Genesis Rabbah*. He felt that not only may people enjoy the benefits of this world – they act improperly if they fail to enjoy the (permitted) fruits of God's creations.

Maimonides' idea

Maimonides (1138–1204, in his *Guide of the Perplexed* 3:17–20) insists that God does not do evil. God is good and everything He produces is good. God created a world to function according to laws of nature. These laws are good. They benefit the world as a whole. People may think that something that happens is bad because they focus on themselves and do not see that in the larger picture, what occurred is good for the world as a whole.

True, a storm or earthquake may kill people, but scientists will testify that these phenomena are natural/healthy for the earth. Bad, explains Maimonides, may occur either (1) because of the impact of the laws of nature upon an individual, as we explained, or (2) because of something that someone else or society or the State did to the person, or (3) because of something the person did to him or herself.

An example of the second is when someone hits another or steals the other's belongings. An example of the third is when a person overeats or fails to exercise his or her body and becomes sick.

Enjoying this world

Maimonides discusses the issue of enjoying this world in his introduction to the *Mishnah Pirke Avot* that he called *Shemoneh Perakim*. In chapter 4, he informs us that proper conduct is a balance between two extremes, both of which are wrong, one is an excess and the other a restriction. Gluttony, for example, is an extreme of excess eating, while abstention from foods is an extreme restriction.

Maimonides tells us that the intermediate path, the "golden mean," is the way a person should behave. People can acquire this good quality by training themselves to act properly, by repeating the deed many times, by "developing habits of good behavior." Thus, in the example of eating, a person should not abstain; he should enjoy good food; but he should not overeat or under eat. In his relations with others, to cite another example, rashness is excess, timidity is restriction, and the "mean," the virtuous act, is to be good natured.

Maimonides cites many proofs for this view, including statements from the Bible, the prophets, the Midrash about the Nazir, and the statement in the Jerusalem Talmud, *Nedarim* 9:1. In the Talmud, a sage criticizes one who adds stringencies to his life that are not prohibited by the Torah: "Is it not enough for you what the Torah has forbidden?!"

Thus Maimonides responds affirmatively to the question, may we enjoy life in this world? "If a person always evaluates his actions and trains himself to perform according to the mean, he will reach the highest level that a human can attain. By doing so, he will draw close to God and understand His will."

Summary

The ancients did not agree on the subject of why bad happens to good people and whether we can enjoy life in this world. In fact Midrashim and sages expressed diametrically opposed positions. It is possible that the negative stance was prompted by historical occurrences; and the rabbis consoled the people during the period of Roman persecution by telling them that they will yet have peace and joy in the world to come.

Parallelisms in the Jacob and Joseph stories

One way to enjoy and understand Scripture is to compare and contrast the wording of one biblical passage or story with another. There are many parallels in the stories of Jacob and his son Joseph.

Questions
1. What is the value of parallels?
2. What are some of the similarities in the lives of Jacob and Joseph?

Value of parallel lives
The famous Greek sage Plutarch, who was born around 50 of the Common Era and died around 130, wrote several books of parallel lives of famous Greeks and Romans. In his still enjoyable volumes, he compared the biographies, the thinking and behavior, of great statesmen, soldiers and orators of the two nations. The well-written portraits were composed with an ethical purpose. They offer inspiring and instructive pictures of notable, indeed heroic figures of antiquity, concrete portrayals of prominent and remarkable lives that Plutarch felt deserve, at least in part, to be emulated. He recognized that the methodology of presenting the resemblances in lives tends to concentrate one's attention to certain behaviors. They prompt the reader to think about what he is reading and model their own life accordingly.

The parallel lives of Jacob and Joseph
The Bible's parallel lives of Jacob and Joseph, composed more than a millennium before Plutarch's magnum opus, also has, among other purposes, a goal to inspire and instruct: to encourage the reader to emulate the good behavior and avoid that which is harmful. The stories are written in a simple very readable style. They bring out the personality and motivation of Jacob and his son. We will list some ways that the two patriarchs are alike. Some of the

resemblances are produced by using the same word in both stories. Others show the similarity and even exact repetitions in their behavior. The match in the stories of the two patriarchs is highlighted by including twin episodes within the Joseph episode itself.

1. The story of Jacob and Joseph begins with the words "and Jacob dwelt" and ends with the identical verb "and Joseph dwelt," as a clear and conspicuous frame to emphasize the relationship of the two stories.

2. Similarly, the Bible draws attention to the fact that Jacob settled "in the land where his fathers dwelt, in the land of Canaan." Both Jacob's and Joseph's lives end when they tell their relatives that they want to be buried there.

3. At the beginning of Joseph's tale, Jacob's sons, Joseph's brothers, are described as shepherds of flocks. The brothers want to separate Joseph from the family. Toward the end, the Egyptians refuse to eat with them because they are shepherds, for this profession disgusts them. Likewise, when Jacob and his family came to settle in Egypt, they had to live apart from the Egyptians.

4. Joseph's narrative starts in Jacob's home with a dream involving the harvest, and ends with a famine of the harvest in Egypt. It continues with a dream about the sun, moon and stars; and later, in Egypt, Joseph presents himself to his brothers as an astrological diviner.

5. Jacob's life begins with the difficulties that he has with his brother Esau and Joseph's with his problems with his brothers. In both, the parents fail to help resolve the sibling rivalry, and may even aggravate it.

6. Joseph is described as resembling Jacob's beloved wife Rachel. The identical words are used for both "shapely and handsome."

7. Jacob was tricked and did not see that Leah was substituted at the wedding ceremony for his intended wife Rachel. The resemblance between Rachel and Joseph apparently deepened Jacob's love for Rachel's son Joseph and may have blinded him from seeing that he was not treating Joseph properly.

8. Jacob and Joseph are younger brothers striving with and prevailing over their elder sibling(s). This contrasts with the behavior of the other people of the time who gave preference to the first born child.

9. Jacob and Joseph are separated from their families for twenty-two years because of sibling strife.

10. The two spend part of the twenty-two years in work that approximates slavery and imprisonment.

11. They are both reunited with their siblings in an emotional reunion and both reunions are accompanied with tears.

12. Jacob makes his sons, Joseph's brothers, jealous by treating Joseph differently. He gives him a distinctive gift, a robe of many colors. Joseph also hands his full brother Benjamin a similar distinctive preferment, five changes of clothing, while he presented his half brothers only a single suit.

13. Love is an element in both accounts and in both it leads to strife and enslavement. Jacob loves Rachel and agrees to work for her father to obtain her as his wife. He is later deceived and is forced to labor an additional slave-like seven years for her. His other wife Leah is aggravated by his special love for her. Later, he shows his love for Joseph and this provokes the anger of his other sons and to Joseph being enslaved.

14. There are many other parallels. For example, chapter 38, the brief episode of Judah and Tamar, which does not seem to concern Joseph at all, is placed in the middle of the Joseph narrative to highlight the similarities and differences between the behavior of the two of them. For example, how each reacted to temptation. Additionally, Judah deprives his father Jacob of a son and later looses two of his own sons. Also, Judah was involved in exiling Joseph from his family and in chapter 38 he lives apart from his family.

Summary

One of the many ways to understand Scripture is to look at it as a literary text. We noted over a dozen parallels between the stories of Jacob and his son Joseph. These parallels were without doubt inserted into the stories to prompt us to think and to derive lessons how we should behave. Jacob and Joseph, like all biblical figures, had faults, but these faults did not destroy their lives. Both, like all human beings, can and should correct their mistakes, act properly and be righteous.

Parallels and differences between the biblical story of Joseph and Homer's Odyssey

There are significant similarities and differences between the biblical tale of Joseph and Homer's classic the Odyssey. By comparing the two remarkable narratives, certain striking facts are brought to light. These facts highlight the moral underpinnings and consequences in the Joseph story.

Questions
1. What are the similarities between the Odyssey and the story of Joseph?
2. What are the differences?
3. What do the similarities and differences teach us?

The Odyssey
The Odyssey was treated as a Bible by the Greeks. Many memorized it and cited it as a guide to life's problems. The mystically and religiously minded Greek philosopher Plato (427–347 B.C.E.) mentions it repeatedly in many of his philosophical treaties. He employs it with the same respect that a modern might use in quoting the Bible. It is one of the two great epic poetic masterpieces of Greek literature that are generally believed to have been composed by Homer (dated as early as the tenth century B.C.E.). The Iliad chronicles the spitefulness of Achilles during the last of the ten year battle at Troy. The Odyssey recounts the ten year journey home of one of the battle's survivors, Odysseus.

Similarities between the Odyssey and the story of Joseph
The life of both Odysseus and Joseph are remarkably alike in many respects, yet significantly different in their moral atmosphere and depiction of character.

1. Both men are the principal personalities in their story. They are portrayed as heroic scions of distinguished families, examples of noble and honorable qualities.

2. Each is absent from the security of his home for about twenty years.

3. The two protagonists make a conscious decision to remain away from their father's land for at least part of their absence, Odysseus at the beginning while he is a leader fighting against Troy and Joseph at the end while he is a leader saving the Egyptians and surrounding nations from starvation. Both periods of time are spent in foreign countries and both last about ten years.

4. The two tales narrate their extraordinary adventures during the years they were missing from their native soil.

5. Both heroes spend some of their period of absence controlling the events of their lives, while losing control during several other years.

6. Part of each of their time away from home is spent in slavery.

7. Joseph and Odysseus are sexually harassed.

8. Odysseus descends into the dark environs of Hades and Joseph into a prison pit.

9. The plots direct our attention toward the moment when each will be reunited with his family.

10. The two manly heroes uncharacteristically cry at the moment of reunion with their family.

11. Clothing is an element relating to personality and relationships in both adventures, although the use and the result of the use are different. The coat of many colors spotlights Jacob's special love for Joseph and is the cause of Joseph's brothers' enmity. Beggar garments are used by Odysseus to hide his identity.

12. Both employ disguises. Odysseus, as mentioned, camouflages himself as a beggar so that his wife's suitors would not recognize him. Joseph conceals his identity by speaking through an interpreter so that his brothers would not hear that he spoke their language and begin to recognize him.

Differences in the two narratives

Despite the similarities, there are striking differences. The dissimilarities draw attention to the distinctive moral attitudes of the two stories.

1. The Odyssey is a tale that extols warfare, the protagonist's behavior in battle and orgiastic alcoholic celebrations. The more aggressive the Greek behaves the higher he is praised. Even some six centuries later, as late as about 350 B.C.E., Plato wrote in his volume *Laws* that in Sparta and Crete the edicts aimed to promote courage in war. He felt that war was wrong. However, he extolled alcoholic drinking parties as good training in temperance. The Bible, on the other hand, is relating a family struggle, and no matter how one interprets Joseph's behavior – even if one insists that he should have treated his family better – it never glorifies war or character training through parties.

2. Gods play a role in the Odyssey, participating on both sides of the conflict and provoking much of it. There is no obvious divine act in the Joseph story. Instead, Joseph is described as making his own decisions.

3. The gods in the Odyssey are depicted as beings with all too human traits who see the earthly creatures as an assortment of playthings upon a stage created to gratify their needs and to amuse them. God in the Bible is a teacher of morality.

4. Homer's world is filled with superstition and the unnatural. No reader of the episodes could possibly face similar circumstances. The biblical tales, in contrast, are stories of problems and reactions to predicaments that are still faced by many people today. A Bible reader sees how wise people handled their situations and the outcome of their acts, sometimes good and sometimes bad, and one can learn from the reading.

5. A key element in both Homer dramas is revenge. While Joseph was mistreated and could have also responded in a revengeful manner, he did not do so.

6. Odysseus solves his problems by killing his enemies, the suitors of his wife Penelope. Joseph, instead, reconciles with his brothers and even supports them.

7. In Homer's works the Greek shows his manliness by taking a woman when and how he desires. His enemies show their manliness by doing what they can to retrieve or revenge the woman. This disparaging attitude to women – treating them as property – is not found in the Joseph story.

8. Odysseus repeatedly surrenders to sexual enticements and other passions but Joseph does not.

Summary

Odysseus' legacy is the glorification of revenge and the notion that the hero is able to overcome his difficulties with might in an immoral "manly" manner. The story of Joseph is entirely different. The relation of Joseph and his brothers and the manner in which their father Jacob handled the family rivalry may be compared with modern family problems. The stories teach us how to behave. Even those who insist that both Jacob and Joseph could have acted differently and not caused the family breakup, recognize that we can learn from their behavior and avoid acting as they did.

Unlike the characters of the Odyssey, the Bible teaches us not to shift the blame for our problems on God or passively seek to have God resolve them or try to settle them by immoral means. It encourages people to work to solve life's difficulties in a proper moral manner, using their abilities. It prompts everyone to realize that acts can set a train of events in motion that could have a long and devastating effect.

Joseph's brothers wanted to enslave Joseph. They succeeded, but they were blind to the dire consequences of their behavior. Joseph's entry into the stratosphere of Egyptian life eventually prompted his brothers to follow him to Egypt. Their stay in Egypt ended in the enslavement of their children for hundreds of years. The years of enslavement, in turn, scared their descendants. It left them with a slave mentality, which Moses was never really able to help them overcome, despite many efforts and a forty year stay in the desert waiting out the death of a generation suffering from psychological enslavement.

*   *   *

"Better to die upright than to live on your knees" is a good proverb, but not a good slogan with which to arrange one's life. A far better guide are the words of Psalm 37:27, "Turn away from evil and do good, and [you will] dwell [in security] forever."

Vayechi

Different possible interpretations of the biblical text

Many claim, with loud enthusiastic (even, occasionally, boisterous) confidence, that they know, and can relate, the exact meaning of a particular biblical passage. These claimants are incorrect. The truth is that many different interpretations of the Bible exist.

Of the commentators: some focus on the past, others on the future, and still others on the present. Some commentators and scholars read the biblical passages rationally, others mystically, and still others pragmatically. Some commentators seek and find an idealistic or even messianic teaching in the biblical text. Frequently, even that which is often thought to be the basic accepted translation of the Torah text, differs from scholar to scholar.

Questions
1. What is the traditional view on the subject of the diversity of biblical interpretations?
2. What is the meaning of Jacob's statement in *Genesis* 49:10?

Multiple interpretations are allowed and expected
The *Midrash Numbers Rabbah* 13 reports that "there are seventy faces to the Torah." Rabbinic literature uses the number seventy in phrases such as seventy nations and seventy languages, where it clearly intends something numerous – nations and languages. Thus the Midrash is alerting us that, contrary to the popular view, there are numerous, even conflicting, allowable Bible interpretations.

The meaning of *Genesis* 49:10 is disputed among the commentators
There are many different interpretations of *Genesis* 49:10.

The passage reveals Jacob's prophecy concerning his fourth son Judah, "The scepter shall not depart from Judah, nor the staff from between his legs; *ad ki yavo shilo*, the obedience of the people shall be his."

The overwhelming consensus among the commentators is that Jacob is not describing his son, but prophesying what will befall the tribe of Judah. Jacob is forecasting that his son's descendants will rule over the other tribes. The reign is symbolized by the metaphors "scepter" and "staff," both symbols of rulership.

Jacob assures his son that the other tribes will accept and be obedient to this king. He seems to foretell that the rule will end *ad ki yavo shilo*. The phrase is obscure. It could be translated "until he comes to *shilo*" or "until *shilo* comes." But what is *shilo*?

All the biblical commentators try to interpret Jacob's intention, but they disagree on the meaning of this phrase.

Rashbam – *shilo* is the city of Shilo and Jacob is referring to the united kingdom of Judah

Rashbam (c. 1080–1158) contends that the phrase refers to Judah's descendants David and Solomon. They would govern the entire Israelite nation, all twelve tribes, until the death of Solomon. At that time, the northern ten tribes would reject the regime of Solomon's son Rehovam, and would select Jerovam of another tribe as their king. This would occur when Rehovam came to the city of Shiloh, in a failed attempt to solidify his reign after his father's death.

Chizkunee – *shilo* is not where Rehovam came but which Ahiyah left

Chizkunee (about the thirteenth century) agrees that Jacob is referring to the end of the Davidic leadership over all twelve tribes and that *shilo* is the city Shiloh. However, he insists that Shiloh is the city from where the prophet Ahiyah came, when he appeared with a prediction before Jerovam (in *I Kings* 11:30). Ahiyah ripped his clothes into twelve pieces and told Jerovam to take ten pieces as a symbol of the ten tribes that he will soon tear off from the Davidic dynasty and control.

David Kimchi – the facts of the others are correct, but *shilo* means "son"
David Kimchi, also known as Radak (c. 1160–1235) interprets *shilo* as "David's son." He derives his view by translating *shilo* as "afterbirth."

Joseph ibn Kaspi – no, *shilo* means "error" and the king is Zedekiah
Joseph ibn Kaspi (thirteenth century) rejects the views of Rashbam, Kimchi and Chizkunee and insists that Jacob is speaking about the end of the last Judean king, centuries later. Kaspi defines *shilo* as "error," the meaning it has in *II Samuel* 6:7.

He defines the verb *yavo* not as "come" but "occur," and states that *ad* "until" denotes when the rule will cease. Jacob is prophesying that there will be Davidic kings until (*ad*) there occurs (*yavo*) an error (*shilo*).

This error occurred during the reign of King Zedekiah, the last reigning king of David's line, who erroneously and foolishly rebelled against the superior army of Babylon. The Babylonians defeated the Judean forces, destroyed the Temple, and "Judah was carried away captive out of the land" (*II Kings* 25:21).

Abraham ibn Ezra – yes, *shilo* is the city of Shilo, but the prediction is about the beginning of David's reign
Abraham ibn Ezra (1089–1164) took an entirely different approach. He read Jacob's words to Judah as a description of the start of David's government, not its end. He interprets *yavo* as the "end" or "destruction" of the city of Shiloh, which occurred during the time of Samuel, close to the beginning of David's reign.

Saadiah – *shilo* means "his" and the verse refers to the Messiah
A most remarkable interpretation is the one held by most of the commentators, although they differ in how they derive their understandings.

There is no mention of a Messiah in the Bible. The term *mashiach*, anointed one, refers to the king or priest. Nevertheless, the *Midrash Genesis Rabbah,* other Midrashim, the Babylonian Talmud *Sanhedrin* 98b, *Targum Onkelos, Targum Pseudo-Jonathan, Targum Neophyti,* Saadiah, Rashi, Nachmanides and others understand that Jacob is speaking to his son about the Messiah.

How did these sources reach their conclusion? Saadiah (882–942), for example, derives this interpretation from a new definition. He reads *shilo* as if it were written *shelo*, "his." He contends that since the Jewish kingdom will ultimately belong to the Messiah, this is the one to whom "his" is referring. He and the other commentators are saying that David's descendants will reign until the Messiah comes.

However, we know that this is not true. The Davidic dynasty ceased in 586 B.C.E. when the first Temple was destroyed. Furthermore, during the second and first centuries before the Common Era Judea was ruled by Hasmonean kings who were not from the tribe of Judah. However, these commentators may be suggesting that Jacob was speaking about the right of kingship. The Hasmoneans usurped the right of David's family. No one has the right to rule as king over the Jews other than from the Davidic family.

Sforno – *shilo* means "boundary" and "peace," bounded before the arrival of the Messiah and peaceful when he came

Sforno (fifteenth century) gives still another variation of the messianic interpretation of *ad ki yavo shilo*. Jacob was speaking about the period when the Jewish state would exist. He did not address the possibility of Jewish statehood being lost. The word *shilo* means "boundaries" and also "peace." Sforno contends that Jacob is predicting that the Davidic dynasty will be "bounded" until the Messiah, the "peaceful" one, will arrive. Then all nations will subordinate themselves to him and he will have power over everyone.

Summary

There are many divergent explanations of biblical texts. Jewish tradition realizes divergences exist, encourages them, and differing opinions are accepted. Thus, the numerous interpretations of an important passage like *Genesis* 49:10 should not be surprising. Not all of the differing opinions were enumerated above – many more exist. The commentators disagree on what Jacob was foretelling his son Judah, how they understand Jacob's words, and how their conclusions were drawn. These few examples reveal that no one should or could state, with any reasonable degree of certainty, that they know exactly the meaning of each biblical verse.

Shemot

If it is easy, it is probably wrong!

The book of *Exodus* launches the narration of the difficult, frequently frustrating story of the foundation of the Israelite nation. The family had been called Hebrews *(ivrim)* by others until now, probably because they came from the other side of the Jordan *(ever hayarden)*. Now they called themselves *b'nei yisrael*, which means "children of Israel" or "Israelites," because they insisted on remembering that they were descendants of Jacob, who was also called Israel. Later, after the return of a remnant of the people from their exile in Babylonia to the area of Judea they were called "Judeans" or "Jews" for short, because most, but by no means all, of them were from the tribe of Judah.

The struggles reported in *Exodus* and the remaining parts of the Bible depict a nation that all too frequently failed to respond maturely to their difficulties and sank, instead, into moods of defeat, depression, passivity and rejection of their divine role.

Questions
1. What do the struggles of the Israelites tell us about our own struggles?
2. Is this lesson also found elsewhere in the Bible?

All beginnings are difficult, and if it is easy it is probably wrong
There should be no doubt that one of the messages of the tales of the Israelites is to teach us not to repeat their type of behavior. It instructs us that all beginnings are difficult, but one must persevere, for the end can be enjoyable and advantageous.

This fundamental lesson is presented right at the beginning of the Bible. The introductory chapters of *Genesis* can be seen as something more than history. They can be understood as a biblical description of the nature of man.

Maimonides sees *Genesis* 2 and 3 as an allegory

In his second chapter of his *Guide of the Perplexed,* Maimonides (1138–1204) explains the story of the eating of the fruit from the forbidden tree as an allegory. In his first chapter, he states that man's ultimate goal is to use his intelligence to guide his behavior.

Maimonides does not address the meaning of the "punishment" inflicted on Adam and Eve. However, we can extrapolate from Maimonides' thoughts and recognize that here too Scripture is describing the nature of man.

Genesis 3:16–19 describes the "punishment." Briefly stated, God states that women will bear children in pain and men will produce food with the sweat of their brow.

In interpreting the story, we need to realize that it is inconceivable that a just God would punish all future generations because of the misdeed of their ancestors Adam and Eve. The descendants did not commit this wrong. Thus the "punishment" must not be a punishment at all. It is a statement telling us about human nature. The lesson was placed at the very beginning of the Torah so that when people read the episodes that follow, they should read the future biblical sections in the light of the teaching of this section.

The introduction teaches that nothing in this world is worthwhile unless it is attained by hardship. If it is easy, it is probably wrong! The introduction is designed to motivate people to develop goals, work to achieve them, and realize that while it will be hard to do so, they must persevere.

God, in essence, was asking the woman, "What act do you think is the most creative act that you can perform." The woman responds, "Giving birth." God then said, "All good things in this world can only come through pain. You say that giving birth is a great creative act. You are correct. It is a good example. You will only be able to give birth with pain. It is the same with all other creative acts."

Then God turned to man and asked the same question. Man said that he saw his most creative act in gathering food from the earth. God said, "You are correct. You will only be able to do so with the sweat of your brow. Remember this lesson and apply it to your other acts."

Others taught Maimonides' message

Many men and women have learned this lesson, but unfortunately many others have not done so. When the normal and expected hardship occurs, they abandon a project.

The Greek poet Hesiod put the biblical lesson this way.

> Wickedness can be had in abundance easily:
> Smooth is the road and she dwells very near.
> But in front of virtue (God has) put sweat:
> Long and steep is the path to her
> And rough at first;
> But when you reach the top,
> Then at length the road is easy,
> Hard as it was.

No man, no country, has been successful without climbing this long, steep, rough road.

The Israelites failed to understand

The Israelites did not learn this introductory lesson. Over and over in the days of Moses and afterward, whenever hardships appeared, they cried out in bitter frustration, blind to the success that perseverance could have brought them.

The message seen in the history of the United States

If the founders of the United States would have had the same attitude, the country would never have been founded. In 1776, the year that the Continental Congress issued the Declaration of Independence, the battles for independence, led by George Washington, were unsuccessful. In a three month period, he lost four battles and anticipating another defeat he gave up one fort without a fight. Washington's second-in-command, his trusted confidant, and many others lost faith in him. Thousands of his soldiers abandoned him and flocked to the British camp to express their loyalty. The Continental Congress fled from their dwelling in Philadelphia and two members ran to join the enemy forces. Thomas Paine described the period, the difficulties, the inability of some to face the trouble and pain, and the potential for success:

These are the times that try men's souls. The summer soldier and the sunshine patriot will, in this crisis, shrink from the service of their country; but he that stands it now, deserves the love and thanks of man and woman.

But then, as the year ended, after a long period of despair, Washington and his ill-clad forces crossed the Delaware River in a surprise night attack and won a victory at Trenton. After months of despondency, this became the turning point of the American Revolution. Abigail Adams, the wise wife of John Adams, the second American president, recognized the advantage of difficulties, what many Americans and ancient Israelites – whose story begins in *Exodus* – missed, the tendency of adversity to forge character. "I am apt to think that our later misfortunes have called out the hidden excellencies of our commander-in-chief…. Affliction is the good man's shinning time."

Summary

The bible teaches that all beginnings are difficult, but people must not despair or cease their efforts. As *Exodus* will show, Jacob's descendants were soon enslaved. They had an opportunity to learn from that experience. After He had redeemed them, God repeatedly told the people to remember that they were slaves in Egypt, learn from the experience to treat all people well. However, even when free, they behaved as erst-while slaves. They were crushed by their difficult beginnings and were unable to move forward. They often failed to learn from their experience.

Va'eira

What is a rabbi?

Moses is in the midst of fulfilling the divine mission to liberate the suffering Israelites from the bleak Egyptian bondage in the portion of *Va'eira*. Tradition refers to Moses as *Moshe Rabbeinu,* which can be translated as "Moses our rabbi" or "Moses our teacher."

Questions
1. Was Moses a rabbi?
2. When did the institution of the rabbinate begin?
3. Is the rabbi of today ordained like the rabbi of old?

The origin of the rabbi
Moses was not a rabbi. The institution of the rabbinate began after the destruction of the second Temple in the year 70 of the Common Era. Rabban Yochanan ben Zakkai, the far-sighted spiritual leader of that generation, realized that the Temple-oriented Judaism with its animal sacrifices, the hallmark of Judaism since the days of Moses, had ceased when the Temple was destroyed.

Yochanan ben Zakkai established "Rabbinic Judaism" in its place. This is a Judaism centered in the synagogue, rather than the Temple. Prayers are recited in place of sacrifices. Instead of *kohanim,* "priests," he inaugurated the idea of rabbis, meaning the teachers of the people. He assumed for himself the title "rabban" at that time. The term signified the leading rabbi.

The religious authorities and scholars before Yochanan ben Zakkai were not called rabbi. Hillel who lived at the beginning of the Common Era had no title; neither did any of the sages listed in the *Mishnah Pirke Avot* who lived before the destruction of the second Temple.

Rabbinical functions

The first rabbis were assigned two community functions, a teaching and a court position. We are familiar with the first: the rabbi teaches the traditions of past generations and informs his congregation of the *halakhah*, the Jewish law. The second task, which does not exist today, was the authority to impose certain judicial fines. This job was restricted to the rabbis living in the land of Israel; those outside of Israel had only the first responsibility. The rabbis in Israel were called *rabee* in Hebrew, while those outside of Israel, primarily in Babylon, held the title of *rav*.

The end of semicha, the ordination of rabbis ceases

A rabbi was "ordained" – that is, recognized as a rabbi – by having another rabbi acknowledge that the newcomer was worthy. He "passed on" the role. The Hebrew term for this ordination is *semicha*. In essence, *semicha* is the recognition or certification by one rabbi that another person is also qualified to serve as a rabbi. In the year 415 of the Common Era, another post-Temple institution, the secular community leadership called the patriarchate, was suppressed by the Romans who controlled Israel and its people since the destruction of the Temple. Many, but not all, scholars believe that the *semicha*, the formal tradition of spiritual leadership, was also abolished by the Romans at that time.

Rabbi Dr. Bernard Revel disagreed. He emphasized that despite the cessation of the secular patriarchate, Israel continued to be a vibrant center of learning until the period of the crusades in the eleventh century. He was convinced that it is inconceivable to think that the Israel scholars would relinquish the *semicha* when there were great scholars learning and teaching Torah in the country. Revel argues that when the spiritual leader Gaon Daniel died in Israel in 1062, there was bitter hostile community struggle over the designation of his successor, causing academic instability and stagnation. The crusaders pillaged Israel several decades later and devastated communal life. The *semicha*, which was in limbo, did not survive.

About a hundred years later, the scholars of the twelfth century argued whether *semicha* could be revived. Maimonides (1138–1204) contended that it could be renewed if the Israeli scholars would consent. Other sages disagreed with Maimonides, and, as a result, no action was taken.

In 1528, in the city of Safed in the land of Israel, Jacob Berab gave *semicha* to twenty-five of his students, based on Maimonides' opinion. Later, he ordained an additional four scholars. He wanted to reestablish Israel as the center of Jewry. The idea was well intentioned and timely. Jews had just been expelled from Spain in 1492 and were seeking a homeland and a place of solace.

However, this rabbi of Safed did not consult the rabbis of Jerusalem before he acted. When they heard what he did, they opposed it. Revel believed that their opposition was not personal: they feared that the reintroduction of *semicha* would precipitate a pseudo-messianic movement. Thus, the practice of the rabbinate instituted by Rabban Yochanan ben Zakkai ceased after the fifth or twelfth century.

Nevertheless, in some countries, such as Italy, France and Germany, teachers started a new idea of issuing a "writ of *semicha*" to their students. This document, like the ancient *semicha,* also certified that in the teacher's opinion the student had the knowledge to teach and function as a "rabbi." The teachers knew, of course, that their *semicha* was not a continuation of the ancient ben Zakkai institution, but they felt that the times required something similar, and it was appropriate to give the new activity the name used by the custom of old.

However, countries such as Spain and other Sephardic lands did not renew the *semicha.* There was no "ordination." As a result, they had no rabbis until the present day. They called their knowledgeable students and religious leaders *chakham*, "knowledgeable ones."

Summary

Moses was not a "rabbi." The institution of the rabbinate began in the first century of the Common Era, after the destruction of the second Temple, when Rabban Yochanan ben Zakkai initiated the practice as a substitute for the Temple service. A rabbi was a teacher who received his authority from a previous rabbi, who passed it to him by means of *semicha* (placing the authority on another). The Romans forbid Jews from continuing *semicha*, according to one view, in the sixth century. According to another it was the crusaders in the eleventh century who stopped *semicha*. Rabbis of today are certainly rabbis, but they do not hold their authority in an unbroken line from the time of the beginning of the rabbinate in the first century of the Common Era.

Is the law of *tefillin* in the Torah?

Maimonides, in his *Book of Commandments,* lists the laws of the *tefillin* (phylacteries) of the head and the *tefillin* of the arm as the twelfth and thirteenth commands, respectively, two of the 613 biblical commands.

Questions
1. What is the source for the idea that there are 613 commandments?
2. What are the commands?
3. What is the source of the *tefillin* law?

The source for the idea of 613 commandments
There is an early fourth century C.E. tradition, a *derasha,* "sermon," of Rabbi Simlai, recorded in the Babylonian Talmud, *Makkot* 23b, that the Torah contains 613 commandments, 248 positive and 365 negative commands.

Identifying the commands
Abraham ibn Ezra
Ibn Ezra (1089–1164) belittled the notion of 613 commandments. He said that if we counted every time that God issued a command in the Bible the count would exceed a thousand. If we numbered only the commands applicable today, the result would be far less than 613. His opinion was rejected and the sermon of Rabbi Simlai was accepted as authoritative.

Cairo
The first attempt to identify the commands did not occur until the second half of the eighth century by Rabbi Simon Cairo in his *Hilchot Gedoloth.* His pioneering act did not fit the scheme outlined by Rabbi Simlai. It contained some ordinances that were obviously of Rabbinic origin, such as the kindling of the post-biblical Hannukah lamps. He was also only able to find 265 positive

and 348 negative commands, numbers that did not correspond to Rabbi Simlai's count. However, Rabbi Cairo stimulated others to begin to enumerate the Torah commands.

Maimonides

Maimonides (1138–1204) scrutinized Cairo's commands and the various lists that followed Cairo's and created his own in *The Book of Commandments*. This work served as an introduction to his *magnum opus*, the fourteen volumes of *Mishne Torah*, where he details and explains the commands.

While he criticizes Cairo severely for including rabbinical commands, it is arguable that he may have also done so himself. For, as we will see, not everyone agreed that the law of *tefillin* ("phylacteries") is biblical. However, it seems clear that Maimonides' approach was to include all the commands that the talmudic rabbis considered to be biblical, even when others might think of them as being rabbinical in origin.

Tefillin
Maimonides

Maimonides derived the Torah command of the *tefillin* of the head from the four-fold mention of "and they shall be for *totaphot* between your eyes." The law is in *Exodus* 13:9, 16, *Deuteronomy* 6:8 and 11:18. He found the command of the *tefillin* of the arm in the four-fold repetition of "you should bind them for a sign upon your hand" in *Exodus* 13:1, 16, *Deuteronomy* 6:8 and 11:18. The sages considered the head and arm *tefillin* to be two biblical commands in the Babylonian Talmud, *Menachot* 44a.

Rashbam

The rationalistic Bible commentator Rashbam (c. 1080–1158), a grandson of Rashi, rejected the idea that Scripture is speaking about *tefillin* in these verses. In his commentary to *Exodus* 13:9, he interprets *totaphot* as "a precious jewel that one places on one's forehead as a decoration." He states that the phrases "*totaphot* between your eyes" and "a sign upon your hand" are biblical metaphors that mean "you should never forget what I am saying. You should remember My teaching as if it is set [between your eyes] and inscribed on your hand. We find a similar phrase [with a similar intention] in *Song of Songs* 8:6, '[one lover says to the other,] place it on your heart as if it had been engraved there like a seal.'"

Ibn Ezra and Chizkunee also recognize that the simple meaning of these scriptural statements is as Rashbam understood them. All three emphasize that we should accept the *tefillin* teaching of the rabbis: we should observe the law of *tefillin* even though they felt that it is a rabbinical practice and not a Torah command.

A reading of the biblical verses supports Rashbam's interpretation. *Exodus* and *Deuteronomy* use the metaphors in different passages, for different purposes, but always as a figure of speech to encourage memory. *Exodus* uses it to exhort the Israelites to remember the deliverance from Egyptian slavery. *Deuteronomy* has it in the mandate to remember to love God. (In *Exodus* 13:9, the bible uses *zikaron*, "a reminder," rather than *totaphot*, but both have the same intention: to remember.)

The meaning of the passage that the rabbis used to support their teaching about the *tefillin* can be seen by looking closely at the details of what is said. In *Deuteronomy* 6, for example, the Bible tells the Israelites that they should employ nine aids to help them remember. (1) They should repeat the command to love God to their children. (2) They should talk about it while sitting at home and (3) when they are out walking and (4) when they lie down and (5) when they get up. Then follows four figurative statements. (6) The teaching should be a sign upon their hands and (7) *totaphot* between their eyes. (8) They should write it on the doorposts and (9) on the city gates. The last two obviously mean that one should also remember to love God whenever one enters or leaves one's home and whenever one enters and leaves one's city.

There are midrashic statements that support Rashbam's reading of the text. The *Midrash Leviticus Rabbah* 22:1 recognizes that the law of *tefillin* is not explicit in the Torah, but states, in essence, that it is a development of Sinaitic law. It reads: "Even things that appear to you to be additions to the actual revelation – for example, the laws of fringes, *tefillin* and *mezuzot* – are also included in the revelation…. And even what a faithful disciple would say in the future to his teacher, were all communicated to Moses at Sinai."

The *Midrash Ecclesiastes Rabbah* 1:10 asks why it was not communicated at Sinai: "Why have you not told us [this teaching of *tefillin*, etc., already]?" It answers: "One must wait for the proper time," most likely suggesting that future social conditions determine when and how the law will be developed.

Leibowitz

While Rashbam thought that the Torah does not contain the laws of *tefillin*, the belief that the laws of *tefillin* are rabbinical in origin does not belittle the command or suggest in any way that it should not be observed.

The twentieth century scholar Yeshayahu Leibowitz (1904–1994) wrote in his book *Accepting the Yoke of Heaven* that most people fail to understand the relationship between the oral and written Torah. He rejects the notion "among the naïve, and sometimes among those who pretend to be naïve, that the entire world of the Torah is nothing but the authorized interpretation of the written Torah."

> What is unique about halakhic ("Rabbinic") Judaism is that it recognizes the autonomy of the oral Torah… in truth it is the oral Torah which is the one which determines and decides and rules, based on its own criteria. And the authority of the oral Torah to rule based on its own criteria is a basic principle of faith in the historic Judaism of the Torah and *mitzvot*, for it is not the literal meaning of the (Bible) verse which guides the Jew in observing the Torah and the *mitzvot*, but the world of the oral Torah

Summary

It should bother no one that the law of *tefillin* is not explicitly mentioned in the Torah, nor, on the other hand, should anyone be bothered by Maimonides including it and other such laws in his list of the 613 biblical commandments. Maimonides counted commands that the talmudic rabbis felt were biblically commanded or that the rabbis believed were inspired by or developed from biblical verses. The idea that *tefillin* is oral law does not demean its importance or diminish its authority; for, as Leibowitz points out, Judaism is not controlled by the biblical text, but by how the rabbis understood it and their received tradition.

Beshalach

Can war be just?

It is the general consensus that the Romans prohibited the Jews in the second century of the Common Era from studying or even reading the five Books of Moses. This affected the long-standing custom – said to have been initiated by Moses himself – of reciting the Torah during the Shabbat services.

Ever ingenious, the Jews circumvented the ban somewhat by reading a portion from the prophetical books. They selected a section that resembled the Sabbath Torah portion in some way. The recital reminded them of the proscribed Torah portion. They called these prophetical passages the *haphtarah*.

Thus, on the Shabbat of *Beshalach*, when the Torah reading includes the song that Moses and the Israelites sang when they witnessed their victory against the Egyptians, the *haphtarah* is the song of Deborah, from the story of Deborah in *Judges* 4 and 5, that Deborah and the Israelites sang when they defeated the Canaanites.

Chapter 4 of *Judges* describes how Deborah, a prophetess and judge, summoned Barak to assemble troops to wage war against the Canaanites who had been subjugating them and treating them cruelly. She tells Barak that this is God's command. After some discussion, Barak does as God willed and the Israelites are successful.

Questions
1. When can a war be just?
2. Was the war by Deborah just?

The preemptive strike
The subject of a just war is complex. We will examine one aspect of it, the preemptive strike. Was Deborah correct that God wanted the Israelites to initiate a preemptive strike? If we take the story literally, Deborah heard God's

command. But the question still remains, why did God command the war? Was it just?

There are many incidences of preemptive attacks in the Bible. Arguably, God inflicting plagues on the Egyptians to save the Israelites is one. Certainly, Abraham initiated a surprise preemptive attack in *Genesis* 14 against the kings that captured his nephew, Lot.

Ehod, in chapter 3 of the book of *Judges,* is another. He, like Abraham, deceived King Eglon of Moab and killed him to save the Israelites from glaring cruelty and near slavery. King Eglon had mobilized forces from several hostile nations. He attacked the Israelites, defeated them and settled in the Israelite city of Jericho. Then he forced the Israelites to serve him in slave labor for eighteen years. The Israelites were faced with overwhelming problems. What could they do to save themselves from the overwhelming forces? How could they end their servitude? Would it be right to deceive their enemies and end their enslavement? Wasn't a preemptive strike the only way of saving themselves, a last resort?

After careful consideration, Ehod, a left-handed judge with a crippled right hand, decided that the only course open to him was to kill the king by deception. He took a short sharp dagger and hid it beneath his clothes on his right side. He then went to the king and brought him a gift.

He told the king that he wanted to tell him something secret from God. The king agreed to a private conversation, without suspecting that Ehod carried a dagger. He could not see it. He saw only a crippled man who could not use his right hand.

When the king rose to hear the message, Ehod stabbed him, left the room and locked it. The king's officials thought the king did not want to be disturbed so Ehod had an opportunity to escape. When the officials saw that the king did not leave his room, they broke down the door and found the dead king. But it was too late to catch Ehod.

While they were involved with taking care of the dead king, Ehod gathered Israelite forces and attacked the garrison at Jericho and defeated the enemy forces. Ehod and the Israelites did not enter Moab and did not take land from them. They only reacquired their own land. The Bible concludes the story by telling us that Ehod's actions secured peace for the area that lasted eighty years.

A criticism of Ehod

The author of the commentary to this section in *The Interpreter's Bible* criticizes Ehod and the Israelites and charges them with barbarity.

> Passages like this, when encountered by the untutored reader of Scriptures, cause consternation and questioning. One must see the situation in the light of the times, when the important matter was to help Israel, and the means to do it were not examined or questioned. All through our Jewish-Christian history there has been the temptation to put so high a value upon the end that any means are justified to achieve it.

An answer to the criticism

The Jewish philosopher and Bible commentator Levi ben Geshon, also known as Gersonides, understood the matter more realistically. Gersonides (1288–1344) was the grandson of Nachmanides, but did not accept his grandfather's mystical approach to life. Whereas Nachmanides insisted that everything in life is controlled by God, Gersonides felt that people should make up their own minds and control what ever they can on earth.

Commenting on verse 3:2 of *Judges* – that God did not remove all the nations from Canaan so "that the generations of Israel might learn warfare" – Gersonides maintains that God wanted the Israelites to learn to defend themselves and not rely on divine protection and intervention.

The author of *The Interpreter's Bible* curiously turns a blind eye to the biblical description of the dire circumstances of the Israelites, their eighteen years of abject servitude to a hostile nation, their need for deliverance, and that combat was their last resort. He discounts the fact that Ehod and the Israelites acted with remarkable restraint. He overlooks the requirement for deception because of the overwhelming forces of the enemy. Frequently, as taught by the Chinese military sage Sun Tzu, the best or only military tactic is deception and surprise. It is often the only means to success and it secures the minimum risk of harm to one's forces.

Ehod's goal was to relieve his people from the bind of the Moabite yoke, not to secure a complete victory over his enemy. Thus he did not follow the tactic of the later German military writer Carl von Clausewitz, who taught the principle of continuity: pursue one's enemy with the utmost vigor without slackening the pace for a moment.

Summary
Some wars are necessary. One example is the preemptive battle of self defense, when this is the last resort. *The Interpreter's Bible* criticized the Israelites for fighting against their enemies to save themselves from cruel long-standing bondage. This commentary turned a blind eye to the fact that the Bible described the Israelites performing a proper and restrained act to rescue themselves from slavery.

Why are there two versions of the Ten Commandments?

There are two accounts of the Ten Commandments. One is in *Exodus* 20 and the second in *Deuteronomy* 5. The two differ in more than a dozen instances in the spelling of some terms, added and changed expressions, word order changes, and the insertion of explanations in the Deuteronomic edition.

An example of a modification in spelling is the use of the letter *yud* or *vav* in one but not the other rendering. An instance where words were introduced is "as the Lord your God commanded" inserted into *Deuteronomy*. An illustration of changes is the diverse reasons for the Sabbath in the Decalogues, the use of *shamor* in *Exodus* and *zakhor* in *Deuteronomy*, *eid shaker* in the first version and *eid shav* in the second, and *tachmod* in the first and *taaveh* in the second. A case of an augmentation is the second reason inserted in *Deuteronomy* for honoring one's parents.

Questions

1. If both versions were given to the Israelites by God through Moses, why does one vary from the other?
2. If one version was not a divine revelation, who originated it and why was it composed?

The midrashic and talmudic answer

The *Midrash Mekhilta d'R. Ishmael, Bachodesh* 7, and the Babylonian Talmud, *Shevuot* 20b, address the matter very briefly. Both focus on only one of the many variations, the fact that *Exodus* 20:8 uses the term "Remember the Sabbath day" while *Deuteronomy* 20:12 has "Keep the Sabbath day." Both give the same explanation, but the Talmud is more verbal: "'Remember' and 'keep' were pronounced in a single utterance – an utterance that the [human] mouth cannot utter, nor the ear hear." These early sources posit that both versions were uttered simultaneously and miraculously by God.

The view of Abraham ibn Ezra

Ibn Ezra (1089–1164) cites many difficulties with the talmudic and midrashic view. Among other things, he notes that the sources do not address the problems adequately. There are many differences, not just one. Are these sources implying that God caused the Israelites to hear the diversity in spelling, added words, altered word order, and appended explanations in a single scrambled articulation? This would have had to be an unusual even unnecessary miracle, he states, the like of which is never recorded elsewhere. Why is this miracle not mentioned in the Bible? The Bible implies that miracles were performed for the sake of the people. In this instance, even assuming that such a miracle could occur, it would have been impossible for the people to understand the scrambled communication. This would have defeated the reason for revealing the Decalogue, to communicate divine laws to the people.

Furthermore, he continues, if God wanted the people to know the different wording, He could have stated them one after another, so that they could be understood. Additionally, if God is the author of the Deuteronomic Decalogue, why does it state in *Deuteronomy* 5:15 "as the Lord your God commanded you"? These words seem to imply that this command was given previously. Where was it stated? The only previous mention is in the *Exodus* Decalogue.

Ibn Ezra answers that God originated the *Exodus* Decalogue, but Moses was the author of the Deuteronomic version, not God. He also explains why Moses changed the wording by revealing several scriptural characteristics.

First

Ibn Ezra tells us that, in a general fashion, biblical style varies its presentations, sometimes stating ideas expansively, and other times briefly; but both, the short and the long versions, have the same meaning and purpose. Biblical words are like bodies and its meanings are like souls. Our focus, he says, should be on the soul (the meaning) not the body (the words), for this is how the Bible works. If two texts have dissimilar wording but the two express the same idea, they should be understood as being identical.

Second

The Bible changes how comments and incidents are reported whenever they are repeated. The alterations include the use of dissimilar words, variations in word order, and differences in spelling, additions and deletions. This occurs frequently in Scripture. Despite these differences, the sense of the two is the same. Thus it is unremarkable that one Decalogue version uses one word and the second another. Ibn Ezra understands that when the sages explained that "keep" and "remember" were said simultaneously they were speaking figuratively. They meant that the two words have the same meaning and intent.

Third

Sometimes Scripture adds a reason when it repeats something. For example, when Rebecca told her son Jacob what she overheard her husband Isaac say, she added the words "before God" to inform Jacob that Isaac spoke prophetically. Moses also added explanations when he reiterated the divine Decalogue.

Mistakes in understanding

Ibn Ezra expressed exasperation with people who fail to understand these scriptural characteristics. He emphasized that people who read meaning in differences, such as when one version adds the letters *vav* or *yud* that is not in the other, they are searching for something that the Torah never intended. Both words, no matter its spelling, mean the same. The interpretation of these misguided individuals, he insists, is improper imaginative preaching.

Similarly, many commentators mistakenly see significance in the fact that each of the Decalogues begins with the first person (God speaking) and changes to the third person (someone relating what God said). Those who are accustomed to reading the Bible and understand its style know, he writes, that the Bible usually makes changes of this kind, even in the same sentence. This is done for stylistic and poetic purposes and should not be taken literally. God revealed the entire Decalogue, even the sections related in the third person. Scripture also changes from plural to singular and past to future, and the reverse, in describing the same thing. One needs to recognize this stylistic characteristic, he insists, and not read made up "meanings" into it.

Summary

Thus, ibn Ezra concludes, the *Exodus* Decalogue is the words of God, while the Deuteronomic version is Moses' personal repetition – his reminder to the people of the revelation that occurred forty years earlier. He added some explanations for the commands in his repetition. Although there are many differences in their wordings, this is nothing more than the result of characteristic biblical styles that enhance the presentation, and one can find a multitude of examples of these features in a score of scriptural passages.

Mishpatim

Can there be laws that require no change?

The word *mishpatim* means laws, and the biblical portion of *mishpatim* contains many civil laws that were, according to tradition, passed on by Moses to the Israelites shortly after they were given the Ten Commandments. As Rabbi Ishmael states in the *Mekhilta de Rabbi Ishmael*: "Just as the preceding [the Decalogue] were given from Sinai, so too were these given from Sinai."

Questions
1. Can laws be produced, human or divine, that require no change?
2. When should laws be changed?

Several facts about laws
　　1. Laws are not the end goal of society. They are a means of attaining proper behavior. The ideal group of people, secular or religious, is controlled by an all-wise leader. The leader knows all that should be known and is able to instruct his people on every necessary occasion what behavior or thought is proper for the benefit of society and the individual. Unfortunately, humanity being what it is, no such ideal all-wise person can be found. Thus the most realistic situation is to chose the best leader possible, or the best group of leaders possible, and let them rule/guide by means of law. But there are problems with law.
　　2. Laws cannot determine what is right, best and just for everyone, because every person is different. Some individuals are more intelligent, compliant, moral and self disciplined, for example, and require few restraints. Others, of a different and opposite disposition, need all kinds of restrictions, and perhaps even rules to make sure that they do not even come close to violating the law.
　　3. Laws are also problematical because human life and earthly conditions constantly change. What is obviously right today may be absurd and

even harmful tomorrow because the law fails to address the changed conditions.

4. Changes in the law are difficult because people find it hard to cope with change. They do not know how to deal with either the old or the new law. They accepted the rationale behind the old law and now find it hard if not impossible to abandon what had been a fundamental principal in their lives. If, they ask themselves, the old law is shown to be wrong, how do we know the new law is correct? If changes are being made, and this shows that the old law is wrong, why should we rely on the legislator and accept any of his laws? What behavior must I now adopt to comply with the new law?

An examination of each point
1. Contrary to the view of many, the Torah and its *halakhot* ("laws") are not the end goal, but only the means. The Torah is certainly holy, but it must be understood and used properly. Moses Maimonides (1138–1204) devoted chapters 30 though 50 of his third book of the *Guide of the Perplexed* to explaining the 613 biblical commands. He starts his explanation by telling us that the "principal object of the law is to remove this doctrine [idolatry], and to destroy its traces." He explains that God wanted to remove "error from our minds, and protect our bodies from trouble; and therefore desired us to discontinue the practice of these useless actions." Thus the first purpose of the law is to renounce and relinquish useless ideas and to prepare ourselves to act properly.

What is the proper behavior? What is the goal of the Torah?

Maimonides writes in chapter 31 that "each and every one of the 613 biblical precepts serves to (1) inculcate some truth, to remove some erroneous idea, (2) to establish proper relations in society, so as to diminish evil, and (3) to train [the individual in] good manners and to warn [the person] against bad habits." Thus, Maimonides explains, the biblical laws are "only the means that He employed for His primary [three-fold] objective."

It therefore seems to follow that the pious individual who spends his time studying Torah without involving himself in proper behavior, is mistakenly treating the study of Torah as the goal, while, according to Maimonides, it is only the means to the goal. Such a person is like the carpenter who spends all his time reading the carpentry manual and does not repair the broken table.

2. While many would like to insist that laws, especially divine laws, can be applicable and beneficial to all people, Maimonides recognizes that this is impossible. In chapter 34, he writes that the law "does not take into consideration exceptional circumstances…. It ignores the injury that it could cause a single person…. [It is like] nature whose various forces yield general benefits, but cause injury to others…. We should therefore not be surprised when we discover that the object of the law was not fully realized in every person…. It is impossible to be otherwise."

Jewish law takes cognizance of the fact that the law can improperly hurt an individual by several means. When the Israelites had a king, the king was allowed to use his judgment and ignore the law in deciding cases. Jewish judges are encouraged when appropriate to decide a case based on "mercy" rather than on the strict rule of the law. There is also a concept of *lifnim meshurat hadin*, which simply stated, encourages one in certain circumstances to go beyond the letter of the law.

3. Maimonides also recognizes that people and conditions change and this affects the laws. In chapter 32, he points out that animals and humans develop slowly from infancy into maturity. It is the same with societies and the Jews were no exception. "It is impossible to go suddenly from one extreme to another. Therefore, human nature makes it impossible for a person to suddenly discontinue the things to which he was accustomed." Thus, since the Israelites were accustomed to offering sacrifices, "God allowed these kinds of services to continue." The prophets, he continues, spoke against the sacrifices, because the people misused them in their days.

While recognizing that some laws were instituted (or allowed) because of the conditions of the time, and implying that the laws will need to be changed when conditions change, Maimonides does not openly advocate for or against change and he presents no program for it.

4. This brings us to the final point, the difficulty of people to accept change. This problem has not been resolved. It is complex. It involves not only the human difficulty to handle change, but other matters such as different philosophies of law, the built-in elements of law that address the problem and the interrelationship between what one wants to change and what one wants to

leave as is and the affect that one has on the other. The three major movements of Judaism approach the problem of change differently. Orthodoxy, or at least many of its adherents, accept the need for change, but focus on the problems and suggest that in view of the problems, changes may sometimes be adopted and instituted slowly. Many Reform concentrate on the needs of current society and suggest quick adjustments. The Conservative movement generally takes an intermediate approach.

The biblical portion of *mishpatim* can serve as an example of these four points

The introductory eleven verses of the portion contain a series of laws concerning male and female slaves.

1. Although the Greek philosopher Aristotle looked at his slave owning society and concluded that slavery is proper, no reasonable person today would argue that this is true. The end goal of the biblical laws was just the opposite of what they seemed to state. The rabbis in the Babylonian Talmud, *Kiddushin* 22a, and elsewhere, taught that the laws of slaves were instituted to lessen the authority of the master and ultimately do away with the disgusting practice. The rabbis themselves added requirements of their own to further this purpose. They required the master to give the slave the best food, drink and bedding that he uses for himself. "Hence it was said," they concluded, "Whoever buys a Hebrew slave is like buying a master for himself.'"

2. The slavery laws certainly did not determine what is best for everybody. They required slave labor from the slave.

3. The slave laws recognized that people's attitude and conditions change. In fact, like the laws of sacrifices, discussed above, the practice was allowed by Torah law only because it was impossible to stop it suddenly. The rabbis recognized the need to change and ultimately obliterate slavery.

4. The history of the slow movement of change demonstrates the difficulty involved in producing it. Suffice it to say, that many years passed before the change occurred, but it happened; and it serves as an example that at least some laws need to be adjusted.

Summary

Four characteristics of laws were discussed. Laws are means and not the end or purpose of life. No law can be perfectly good for every person because people differ in personality, intelligence and needs. Laws must change to meet changed circumstances. People have difficulty accepting change.

Terumah

What is the significance of the Ark?

We can understand the significance of the Ark by examining several biblical verses and episodes, especially the story of the capture of the Ark in the days of the prophet Samuel and the prophet Jeremiah's reaction to the feelings of the people during the days preceding the destruction of the first Temple a half dozen centuries later.

Questions
1. What is the significance of the Ark?
2. What is the early history of the Ark?

The introduction of the Ark in Jewish history
Exodus 25 begins the description of the construction of the Tabernacle, which was the "house" of God for several centuries until King Solomon built the first Temple. The central article of the Tabernacle was the Ark, which housed the Decalogue, also called the Ten Commandments.

Exodus 34:27 states that the Decalogue symbolized the relation between God and the Israelites: "by these words I have sealed a covenant with you [Moses] and Israel." The Ark that held it had several names, including the "Ark of Testimony," suggesting that the Ark testifies to the relationship between humans and the deity. *Exodus* 34:10 elaborates and clarifies this covenant: God tells the Israelites that he will drive out the current inhabitants of Canaan if the Israelites do not mix with these nations when they enter Canaan and do not worship their idols.

The promise to grant the Israelites sole possession of the land was contingent upon these two conditions. When the Israelites breached the agreement by mixing with the nations, even intermarrying with them, and worshipped their gods, God was absolved from his part of the agreement. This is like a marriage. At the Jewish wedding ceremony, the groom breaks a glass.

Among other things, this practice reminds the couple that one wrong step in the marriage will break it.

The Israelites were impressed by God's promise of a covenant. This impression apparently prompted them to institute the practice of taking the Ark with them when they were involved in warfare. They simplistically thought that even though they violated the covenant with God, God was still obligated under the agreement to aid them. *Numbers* 10:35 may reflect the use of the Ark in battle: "When the Ark would journey, Moses said, 'Arise Lord and scatter your foes, and let those who hate you flee from before You.'"

Were there two arks?

Scholars differ whether there were one or two arks. If there were two, one Ark carried the first Decalogue that Moses shattered when he saw the Israelites worshipping the golden calf. The second Ark contained the unbroken version. The view that there were two Arks suggests that the Israelites always carried the Ark with the broken Decalogue into battles and only resorted to the other when they were in great distress.

The capture of the Ark

I Samuel 4 tells the story of the Israelites' fight against the Philistines. The Israelites lost the first encounter and felt certain that bringing the Ark to the battle of the second day would assure them success.

The Philistines heard that the Ark would accompany the Israelite forces and were worried. Totally discouraged at first, they were then emboldened by their leaders and decided to counter the problem by fighting more forcibly. Seeing the Philistines' greater effort, the Israelites simplemindedly relied on the Ark and lost. The battle was so decisive that the Philistines even captured the Ark, which had been dwelling in Shilo, and held it for many years.

The word "philistine" is used in modern English to describe one who is looked down upon for lacking culture, for being indifferent to better ideas, and for having thoughts that are commonplace. By relying on something that could not assure success, the Israelites at that time showed that they were philistines. They failed to understand that what "saves" is the observance of the Decalogue that the Ark contained, not the objects that carried the thoughts.

Jeremiah

The prophet Jeremiah made this point in chapter 7 of his book dramatically. The Israelites were being attacked by Babylonian forces. Jeremiah criticized the people for thinking that since they had a Temple God would save them. He emphasized that just as the Israelites relied on bad judgment in Samuel's days and lost the Ark from which they foolishly sought aid, so too the people of his day would lose the Temple unless they acted properly to save themselves.

> Do not trust in the lying words of those who say to you, "the Temple of the Lord, the Temple of the Lord. If you amend your ways and your acts, you will be the Temple of the Lord; if you execute justice between a man and his neighbor….
>
> Therefore, go now to My place that was in Shilo, where I set My name at first, and see what I did to it because of the wickedness of My people Israel….
>
> Therefore, I will do to this house that is called by My name, in which you trust…as I did to Shilo.

The Synagogue Ark

Today, the Ark at the front of the Synagogue is a symbol of the ancient Ark that is no longer in our possession. It contains Torah scrolls instead of the Decalogue. Unfortunately, many people come to the Synagogue and give the Ark and the Torah great respect, standing, for example, when the Ark is opened. But they forget, as their ancestors, that Judaism does not respect objects, but behavior. The significance of the Ark is that it is a symbol of the behavior that Judaism requires.

There is an interesting practice of calling people to the reading of the Torah, rather than simply notifying them before hand and allowing them to come to the Torah reading at the appropriate time on their own initiative, without being called up to it. The practice emphasizes the need for appropriate behavior. The person that participates in the Torah reading is reminded that he is not enhanced by his own initiative. He is part of the community and is called to the Torah reading by the community; and he must consider the community whenever he acts.

Summary

The Ark was introduced to the people as part of the Tabernacle during the days of Moses. The Ark was intended to serve as a reminder of the relationship between the Israelites and God. This relationship, or covenant, required the Israelites to act in certain ways toward God and fellow humans. The Israelites did not do so. Instead, in an almost superstitious manner, although they breached the covenant, they felt they could use the Ark, in a kind of magical manner, carry it into battle with them and expect it to assure them of victory. When they had to fight against the Philistines, for example, they brought the Ark with them, but they lost the war and the Ark was taken from them by the Philistines. The prophet Jeremiah saw the same misguided reliance in his own day and criticized the people for their wrong-headed attitude. The Ark in the Synagogue of today also reminds us not to respect objects, but to act properly.

Tetzaveh

The origin of the Synagogue Sabbath sermon

God commands Moses in *Exodus* 28:3 to speak to the "wise-hearted people, those whom I have filled with the spirit of wisdom" and tell them to make certain vestments for Aaron and his sons so that they can function as priests in an impressive manner in the Tabernacle. Moses passed on God's words and explained them. One could call Moses' instruction a sermon in its simplest form.

Questions:
1. What is a sermon?
2. When did it originate?
3. How did it change?

Sermons are in the Bible
A sermon, simply stated, is a speech usually based on a Scriptural text that transmits spiritual instruction. The goal of the sermon is to urge the listener to adopt proper moral and religious behavior. Moses, of course, was the first sermonizer. He told the Israelites the words of God, explained the words to them, and exhorted them to observe them. The fifth book of the Bible, *Deuteronomy*, for example, is in large part a repetition of some previously-stated laws with Moses' comments upon them and his exhortations, a series of several sermons. The Decalogue in *Deuteronomy*, to cite another example, is, according to Abraham ibn Ezra (1089–1164), different than the *Exodus* version because it is Moses' attempt (sermon) to explain what God had commanded, give reasons for some of the commands and encourage the people to observe them.

Some parts of the biblical books that were written after the Pentateuch, especially the works of the prophets, also expound upon the Pentateuchal laws. The books called *Chronicles*, for example, retell many of the incidences contained in earlier volumes, such as the book of *Kings*. *Chronicles* provides a different perspective of the events, and in some instances a commentary on the earlier book. Therefore, one must say that the origin of the sermon is the exposition of the Torah in the Torah itself. The sermon – and Midrash, as we will see – was, therefore, not a rabbinical invention.

Second Temple period

When the Israelites returned from the Babylonian exile, after the destruction of the first Temple in 586 B.C.E., Ezra the Scribe, one of the Jewish leaders of the period, gathered the people and read the Torah to them, "so they understood the reading" (*Nehemiah* 8:8). How Ezra made the Torah understood is obscure. Some say that this was the origin of the *Targum*, the translation of the Bible into Aramaic. The returning Judeans, raised in Babylon, did not know the language of their exiled parents. However, it is also possible that this was a form of a sermon, an explanation of the Scriptural text. Even if this particular verse does not explicitly refer to Ezra explaining the Torah to his people, it seems certain that he must have explained it, for this generation was so removed from Judaism that they could no longer understand Hebrew.

Post-Temple period

During the second Temple times (516 B.C.E.–70 C.E.), the practice became well-spread that the people outside of Jerusalem gathered in meeting houses, later called Synagogues, to recite prayers and study Torah. One person who was present – for this was before there were "rabbis" – would deliver a discourse, an explanation or elaboration, a proto-sermon, on the biblical reading.

During the second half of this period, various groups began to teach different ideas. One of the groups was the Pharisees who, in contrast to the Sadducees, taught that the Written Torah is supplemented by an Oral Torah. The Sadducees, in contrast, taught that one should not rely on the Oral Torah of the Pharisees, especially since it differed with the plain reading of the Torah text, but use only the Written Torah. Thus, when the Bible stated that there should be no fire in your home on the Sabbath (*Exodus* 35:3), the Sadducees sat in cold dark rooms. The Pharisees insisted that the Oral Torah interpreted these words to mean that one may not ignite a fire on the Sabbath.

The Pharisees saw the Oral Torah as a supplement that explained the Written Torah and told how it should be observed. They derived many of their teachings from the words of the Written Torah by means of *derash*, which means "derived." The word *derasha*, which is drawn from *derash*, is the Hebrew for "sermon," for *derash* is, in essence, a sermon.

It was during this time that the sages began to gather oral collections of interpretations, *derashot*, the plural of *derasha*, which were later assembled into books called Midrashim, a noun that also grew from *derash*. The Midrashim are collections of these sermons by various sages, each having its own approach to the biblical text. They contain both legal (*halakhah*) and fanciful crowd-pleasing interpretations (*aggadah*). The purpose of *derash* and the later midrashim, as the sermon today, was to provide not only a basis for the Oral Torah, but to give the people a knowledge of the basic ideas of Judaism, both ethical and ritual laws and practices.

In the fourth chapter of the New Testament book Luke, Jesus is said to have discoursed on the prophetical reading of the Sabbath in the Synagogue during this period. This could reflect the existing practice. It is consistent with what we know of the behavior in the meeting houses during this age. However, there is no certainty that this is what the Lucian writer intended.

Medieval period

Other Midrash books continued to be written during the medieval era, but the church persecuted the Jews during several of these centuries and made every effort to suppress Jewish practices. During the sixth and seventh centuries, for example, the church forbid sermons. Ever inventive, the Synagogue worshipers created religious poems, *piyyutim*, that the congregants recited or heard the prayer leader chant. The *piyyutim* contained rabbinical teachings that had previously been taught by the rabbi in his sermon.

The persecutions killed the sermon in virtually all the Ashkenazic (European) Synagogues during this time. After the persecutions ended, sermons did not revive as a general practice because most of the medieval rabbis focused their attention on learning and teaching Jewish law, and many were not trained or competent speakers.

The rabbis of the medieval age, as well as some today, preferred to demonstrate their intelligence by expounding esoteric, non-practical elements of Jewish law, rather than giving relevant sermon that would enlighten and inspire the daily lives of the congregants.

These rabbis, until the fourteenth century, were not Synagogue employees, for the rabbis felt that it was wrong to accept payment for teaching Torah. Their need to spend their time and effort in other employment also restricted them from lecturing. However, they did deliver two lectures annually, for about an hour or so each. One was recited on the Sabbath before Passover, and usually focused on the technical laws of the holiday. The second was given on the Sabbath before Yom Kippur and dealt with the issues of sin, repentance and piety.

In some parts of Europe, this dearth of soul-searching and comforting sermons was filled by itinerate charismatic preachers, *maggidim*, with a flair for dramatic parables and folk tales who attracted large audiences as they traveled from town to town and spoke on weekday nights or on Shabbat afternoons. They were paid for their speeches on the week night or after the Shabbat.

This did not affect Sephardic (Spanish, Portuguese, African and Israel) Jews, who did not undergo the same kind of persecution as their European brethren. Preaching sermons continued to be an important element of the Sephardic Shabbat worship.

Modern times

The modern rabbinical sermon became a regular part of the Sabbath services in the 19th century. Since it originated in Reform congregations and copied the pastoral practices of Protestant ministers, many Orthodox rabbis initially opposed the practice. When they finally agreed, many insisted that the sermon be delivered in Yiddish. However, when it was found in the mid-twentieth century that many of the American congregants no longer spoke this language, the sermon was delivered in English.

The new sermons were radically different than those that preceded them. The rabbis of today, like their Protestant counterpart, see themselves as pastors who try to improve the social and mental needs of the congregants.

Often, the rabbis no longer use the 15–20 minutes allotted to them for their sermons in interpreting biblical passage, *derash*, as was done in the Bible, and by their Rabbinic predecessors. This function is left to the teacher in the classroom or to a class that the rabbi or another Synagogue official or member conducts during a time other than the worship services. Similarly, the rabbi of today delivers weekly sermons that generally focus on current events and problems faced by the congregants rather than hour-long discourses in the finer points of Jewish law.

Since the fourteenth century rabbis have been paid for their services and the role of *maggidim* has ceased. Instead, visiting "scholars in residence" are invited on occasions to Synagogues that can afford them. These speakers usually speak at times other than the worship services on subjects that the Synagogue officials or the rabbi thinks would interest the congregants. The scholar in residence might give a lecture on Jewish history or philosophy, a subject that one can not adequately cover during the 15–20 minutes allotted to the sermon.

Summary

Sermons began with the interpretations and explanations that one part of the Bible gave to an earlier statement. Sermons were part of the Synagogue services during the latter part of the second Temple period. The ancient sages taught the Oral Torah by deriving their teaching of how the law should be implemented from the biblical text, even when the text itself did not explicitly state the lesson. The word "derive" in Hebrew is *derash*. A *derasha* is the Hebrew word for sermon. The word Midrash is also related to *derash*. Midrash is a kind of sermon. The sermon was forbidden by the church during the medieval period. When the persecution stopped, the rabbis gave only two sermons a year. Traveling preachers, when available, spoke at other times. The modern sermon did not begin until the 19th century, and was initially opposed by Orthodox rabbis.

*   *   *

Since we mentioned that the early rabbis felt that it was inappropriate to take payment for their services, it might interest the reader to know that according to some scholars the prophets, or at least some of them, may have taken payment, or a tip, for their services.

In *I Samuel* 9:7, Saul discusses with his servant what payment they can bring Samuel when they consult him about lost asses. In *I Kings* 14:3 King Jerovam sent his wife to the prophet Ahiyah with a gift for the prophet, to inquire about the health of his son. In *II Kings* 5:15 the general of Aram Naaman offered the prophet Elisha a large gift for helping remove his leprosy. In *II Kings* 4:42, a man brought Elisha a gift, which Elisha gave to the poor.

The impact of the golden calf upon Jewish history

One of the most significant incidences in ancient Jewish biblical history, an episode that had a momentous impact upon the subsequent history and thinking of the Jewish people, was the unusual and tragic mutiny against God, the worship of the golden calf.

What happened?

God had revealed the Decalogue to the Israelite nation less than six weeks previously in an impressive ceremony. One would think that the Israelites would have been unable to rebel against God after such an awe-inspiring revelation. *Exodus* 19:16–19 describes a morning scene of heavy clouds, thunder and lightning. The powerful sound of a shofar was heard growing louder and louder. Mount Sinai seemed to be burning and smoking. The mountain shuddered. The people trembled at the sights and sounds. *Exodus* 20:15 states that the entire nation saw the flames and the smoking mountain, heard the thunder and the shofar, and were frightened. They retreated trembling from the mountain. Verse 16 describes them feeling that they were going to die. *Exodus* 24:3 recalls that they all listened as Moses told them what he heard from God, and every one of the people promised, "All that the Lord has spoken, we will do."

Moses then ascended Mount Sinai to acquire additional laws from God. He is gone only forty days. He returns and finds the people worshipping a golden calf that his brother Aaron helped make for the people.

Questions

1. How could the Israelites rebel against God by worshipping a golden calf after participating in the revelation at Sinai and being dramatically affected by what they saw?

2. Did the Israelites act with bad intentions?

3. How could Aaron, the future high priest, take part in the idol worship?

4. Why did the Israelites use a calf and not another object?

5. Did the Israelites worship a calf after the days of Moses?

Different interpretations of what happened

There are two approaches to interpreting the behavior of the ancient Israelites. One group of scholars prefers to see the ancestors as holy people who did no wrong. They attempt to explain away every seemingly bad behavior or at least soften it. The other group feels that everyone, even the patriarchs and matriarchs, were human and occasionally acted unsuitably. They suggest that we can learn from the ancients: despite mistakes, they were able to do great things and serve as an inspiration to their descendants. We, they say, can do the same.

According to the first company of scholars, Abraham and Isaac were not dishonest when they told the Egyptians that their wives were their sisters, Jacob did not cheat his brother out of his birthright, Joseph was not behaving vainly, David did not commit adultery, etc. According to the second set, they did not act correctly. Likewise, each of these groups interprets the golden calf episode differently. The first states that the Israelites did not act shamefully, the second that they were shockingly wrongheaded.

Ancestors did not do wrong

The commentators who attempt to acquit the Israelites of guilt or at least soften it, state that the people recognized God, were true to Him and were not attempting to worship idols. Depending on the analyst, they were either seduced by Satan or involved in gaining help through supernatural, astrological or mystical means.

Rashi (1040–1105) believed in the existence of corporeal demons. Relying on the Babylonian Talmud, *Haggigah* 16a, for example, he writes in his commentary to *Genesis* 6:19 that Noah saved the demons in his ark along with his family and animals. In regard to the golden calf, he elaborates on a view mentioned in the Babylonian Talmud, *Shabbat* 89a, and the *Midrash Exodus Rabbah*. He argues that the Israelites were misled by the demon Satan, who scared the people by creating frightening turmoil in the heaven and anxiety-producing darkness, and who told the people that Moses was dead. He even showed them Moses' bier. The non-Israelite mixed multitude, which accompanied the Israelites during the exodus, were the first to be misled. They, in turn, enticed some, but not many, Israelites to join them. They threatened Aaron with death. Aaron tried many tricks to delay them from carrying out their plan to substitute a calf for God. However, Satan harried the people. He was assisted by magicians among the people, who produced the golden calf instantly though their magic.

Rashi's grandson Rashbam (c. 1080–1158) was a rationalist of sorts, but he also believed in the supernatural. He maintains that the Israelites were not trying to make an idol, but a kind of *teraphim*, an item "made by means of witchcraft," which is mentioned in *Genesis* 31 and other places in the Bible. In *Genesis*, Rashbam refers to *Hosea* 3:4 and *Zechariah* 10:2 and states that they were objects that could speak and supply "information to people believing in their power…. They were consulted widely to provide information about the future, information of a supernatural dimension." In *Genesis*, Jacob's wife Rachel took them from her father Lavan so that he would "be unable to locate the whereabouts of Jacob and his family." The *teraphim* had "divine powers, which they could exercise, just as the prophets who performed miracles." The Israelites, believing that Moses was dead, thought that they were using the same divine-like force that helped free them from Egyptian slavery. God, explains Rashbam, repeatedly instructed the people not to rely on witchcraft, even though it works. (This view about the efficacy of witchcraft was shared by Halevi, Nachmanides and others.)

Yehudah Halevi (born around 1080) was influenced, as were most scholars and the masses of his generation, in the effectiveness and usefulness of astrology and magic, which, as we mentioned, he felt Jews were not allowed to use. He contended that in the era of the Egyptian exodus, most people could not think of a deity without a visible representation. Realizing this, God appeared to the Israelites during the exodus in pillars of cloud and fire so that the Israelites would have a visual experience. When Moses ascended Mount Sinai, the people expected him to return with some sacred object that would help them in their worship of God. When he failed to return at the expected time, some, but not all, the Israelites, wanting to worship God as they felt proper, tried on their own to create a substitute image as a replacement for the image that they expected Moses to bring them. The people used magic and astrology to create the object. Thus, according to Halevi, their error was not idolatry, but a violation of the command forbidding the making of images.

Abraham ibn Ezra (1089–1164) also believed in astrology. He explains some of the biblical occurrences as being the result of astrological phenomenon. He was also convinced that no one acted improperly during the golden calf episode. The people thought that Moses had died. They saw him ascend Mount Sinai. They knew that there was no food on the mountain and that the manna did not fall there. They saw that he was gone for forty days, and were certain that no person could subsist without food for so long a period. They expected him to return earlier, for Moses, who did not know how long God would keep him, did not tell them when he would return. Since they were convinced that Moses was dead, they sought leadership through astrology – for the calf, the constellation Taurus, could be used, they believed, to attain astrological aid. The term *Elohim,* which describes the calf, does not denote a god, but something with power, as in *Exodus* 32:1.

Rabbeinu Chananel (born around 975) also contends that the calf was an instrument used to obtain astrological aid.

Nachmanides (1195–1270) believed in demons, the supernatural, magic and astrology and interprets many biblical matters using this belief. However, he was also convinced of the efficacy of mystical acts and was the first biblical commentator to use mysticism to explain the Bible, and does so here. He also insisted that the Israelites were not trying to make a god. They thought that Moses was lost, and they were seeking a replacement leader. Although Nachmanides does not say it explicitly, he was also apparently translating the Hebrew word *elohim*, not as "god," but as an important item, the meaning it has in several biblical verses. Nachmanides contends that Aaron chose the calf as the replacement for Moses since, as indicated in the vision of the divine chariot in *Ezekiel* 1:10, the face of an ox was on it. Nachmanides felt that Aaron wanted to use the figure of the calf in a mystical manner to bring God to help the people.

There were many other attempts to exonerate the Israelites based on supernatural notions. L. Ginzberg, in his *The Legends of the Jews*, cites Midrashim that narrate that the Israelites thought that an ox helped save them from the Egyptians because they saw a vision of the Celestial Throne while they were passing though the divided Red Sea. They noted that one of the creatures on the Throne was an ox. Another Midrash relates that the Israelites saw footprints of angels that assisted them at the Red Sea on the sand at the beach, and the footprints were like those of calves. Therefore, when they were seeking something to help them after Moses' apparent death, they decided to make a golden calf.

Saadiah Gaon (882–942) ignores the previously-mentioned superstitious and mystical explanations. However, he too felt that Aaron did not act improperly. Aaron agreed to build an altar for some individuals who wanted to worship an idol, but it was a trick to identify who among the group that approached him were rebels against God. Similarly, the Midrashim *Leviticus Rabbah* and *Tanchuma* state that Aaron agreed to build the golden calf only after he saw Hur, another Israelite leader, being killed and when he was threatened that he would be killed as well.

The Israelites acted disgracefully

Recalling that the calf incident occurred forty days after the revelation of the Decalogue, R. Ulla in the Babylonian Talmud, *Gittin* 36b, compares the guilty parties to an outrageously unfaithful bride: "How shameful is a bride who has been unfaithful under the wedding canopy [the marriage of the Jewish people to God]."

Some rabbis in some Midrashim accepted the view that the Israelites, or at least some of them, behaved badly in building the calf. The *Midrash Tanchuma* relates that God had decided to give everlasting life to the nation that would accept the Torah. But when the Israelites worshipped the calf, they lost this power and had to study Torah in suffering and bondage, in exile and unrest, with daily cares and its burdens, until the messianic age.

The *Midrash Pirke d'Rabbi Eleazer* narrates that although their husbands acted in a contemptible manner, the Israelite women refused to participate in the event and would not give up their jewelry and gold to be used to construct the calf. God rewarded them by creating a special holiday for women, of the new moon (which is not commonly observed today).

The Midrashim *Leviticus Rabbah* and *Exodus Rabbah* state that God knew that Aaron was motivated by good intentions, therefore He did not withhold the high priesthood from him. However, the former Midrash curiously adds that Aaron nevertheless should not have helped the rebellious group build the calf and he was punished by the death of two of his four sons.

Two philosophers, Philo and Maimonides, explained the misdeeds of the Israelites by their understanding of human nature.

Philo (about 20 B.C.E.–20 C.E.) states that when Moses left his nation and "remained several days alone with God, the fickle-minded among the people, thinking that his absence was a favorable opportunity, as if they no longer had any ruler at all, rushed unrestrainedly to impiety, and forgetting the holiness of the living God, became eager imitators of the Egyptian inventions." The calf that they selected to worship was the popular sacred animal of pagans in the area. They abandoned themselves up to unholy sacrifices, blasphemous dances and strong intoxicating wine.

Moses Maimonides (1138–1204) passionately rebuffed the interpretations of the commentators who attempted to clear the Israelites of any guilt by non-rational means. He strongly rejected the notion of demons, the supernatural, magic and mysticism, and considered such ideas as bordering on idol worship, if not idol worship itself. He insisted on a thoroughly rational approach. He noted that a simple reading of the biblical text reveals that the people acted improperly. Unlike most other scholars, Maimonides stated in his *Guide of the Perplexed* 3:32 that God does not need the Temple and its sacrificial services. However, God knew that humans required physical structures, prayer and sacrifice, rather than intellectual thinking, which He preferred. Recognizing that humans can only change, grow and improve slowly, and preferring not to change human nature by miracles, He "allowed" the Temple services, sacrifices and prayers. The immature, non-rational behavior of the Israelites with the golden calf was a paradigm of the lowest level of human nature, the need to express love to God by non-rational means.

Later use of calves in worship

The calf was worshipped for centuries by the Israelites in a later period. *I Kings* 12:26ff tells the story of Jerovam I of the kingdom of Israel, the nation that split off from Judea after the death of King Solomon. He erected two golden calves in the temples he constructed in Beth El and Dan. Some scholars state that he relied on the *Exodus* story, which seemed to indicate that calves had some sanctity. The calves were placed in the physically accessible courts of the temples where the people could touch them. It is uncertain whether the calves were meant to represent God or were seen as the seat or pedestal upon which the invisible God was thought to stand.

Summary
The unusual story of the golden calf raises many questions. Some of the traditional commentators are convinced that Aaron and the Israelites did no wrong when they built the calf. Most of them base their conclusions on astrology, magic, superstition and mysticism, notions that most moderns reject. Other scholars take the text literally, see the people acting improperly, and use the opportunity to explain what it was in human nature that caused them to act so improperly.

*   *   *

Some scholars, but of course not all, offer an interesting interpretation of *Judges* 17 and 18 – the story of Micah's molten image – that is relevant to our discussion. They contend that the story was written in the southern kingdom of Judea to mock and reproach the Temples of the northern kingdom of Israel. They claim that these two chapters were composed sometime after 732 B.C.E., when the Temples at Beth El and Dan were destroyed by invaders. The chapters, according to them, relate what they considered the repugnant origin of the golden calves that Jerovam placed in his Temples. The story shows that the golden calf at Dan existed for some time before Jerovam and it came to Dan under disgraceful circumstances.

Micah is called Micahu in the opening part of chapter 17. The name means "who is like God." Later, he is called Micah, without the ending signifying God, to allude to the un-godly circumstances of the story.

Micah stole a huge amount of money from his mother who had promised the funds to God. After some time, Micah admitted the theft and returned the money to his mother. She gave it back to him to build a golden image and other objects for his home sanctuary. Micah used part of the funds to build the golden image, but pocketed the rest. Although the text does not identify the type of image that was constructed, scholars state that it was a golden calf. Micah made his son a priest of the home sanctuary, but later, for unknown reasons, replaced him with a Levite for a stipulated annual sum.

Meanwhile, the tribe of Dan was searching for a settlement and dispatched five spies to northern Canaan to reconnoiter the land. The spies happened to spend the night at Micah's estate, met the Levite priest and saw the golden calf and other sanctuary articles.

They left in the morning and found an unprotected non-Israelite city in the north that was easy to conquer. They returned to their brethren and brought a band of 600 warriors to take the unprotected city from its peaceful inhabitants.

The warriors passed Micah's estate and stole the golden calf and other property belonging to Micah. In a sordid fashion, they persuaded the Levite priest to breach his contract with Micah and become a priest to their tribe when they conquered the undefended city. When Micah requested that they return his property, they threatened to kill him and his family if he continued to bother them. The warriors were successful and rebuilt the defeated city, which they named after their tribe, Dan.

The scholars contend, as we said, that the Judean author of this story was making a mocking and disparaging comment on the origin of Jerovam's golden calf at Dan. It was no wonder, the author was saying, that the Temple was destroyed around 732 B.C.E.: it was punished for such a despicable past.

Vayak'hel

The lesson of the Tabernacle: Humans must create

Beginning with chapter 25 through the end of *Exodus*, with the exception of chapters 32–34, the Torah describes the construction of the mobile dessert sanctuary called the Mishkan, the Tabernacle in English. The Israelites used this portable "house of God" as a sacred institution for several centuries until King Solomon built a permanent structure, the Bet Hamikdash, The Temple.

The narration of the construction of the Tabernacle and its utensils follows the story of the revelation of the Decalogue and other laws at Sinai, highlighting its significance for the Israelite nation. The recital repeatedly mentions that the construction followed divine instructions and a celestial pattern. In 25:8 and 9, for example, God commands, "Let them make a Mishkan [a dwelling] for Me so that I may dwell among them. Exactly as I show you – the pattern of the Mishkan and the pattern of the utensils – this is how you should make it."

There are close parallels between the wording and description of the creation of the Tabernacle in *Exodus* and the world in *Genesis*.

Questions
1. What are the similarities between the creation of the Tabernacle and the world?
2. What does this parallelism teach us?

Parallels
1. Both narrations concern the making of something significant with God being involved and expressing approval.

2. Creation concerns the building of the physical world and the Tabernacle the spiritual.

3. Creation ends with the bringing of humans on to the earth, and the Tabernacle with a sense of bringing the divine "among them."

4. There are seven sections in the Tabernacle story introduced by God speaking, paralleling the words of God during the seven days of the formation of the world (*Exodus* 25:1; 30:11, 17, 22, 34; 31:1, 12).

5. Six of the seven sections concern acts of creativity, like the initial six days. The seventh concerns the Sabbath laws, corresponding to the first Sabbath.

6. The erection of the Tabernacle was finalized on the New Year day, as indicated in 40:17, just as the world, according to a talmudic sage, was fully fashioned on this Rosh HaShanah day.

7. The wording of 39:42, 43, describing the completion of the Tabernacle is strikingly similar to those in *Genesis* 1:31 to describe the finishing of creating the world.

8. The verb *vay'chal*, "finished," is used in both 40:33 and *Genesis* 2:2 to describe the conclusion of the two constructions.

9. Moses made a blessing in 39:43 when he put the final touches on the Tabernacle and so does God in *Genesis* 2:3.

Difference

There is a significant difference between the two incidences. God created the world, but humans made the Tabernacle. In 35:4 and other sections, Moses tells the people that God commanded that they must participate in the creation of the Tabernacle. He instructed men and women to bring the best of their goods for the Tabernacle and its utensils.

He was telling the Israelites that the only way to cause God to "dwell among" them is if they make a contribution, an active effort.

The human duty to create with the best that they have

One can reasonably assume that the stories may be compared to teach two lessons. First, God created the world and ceased creating, and it is now the duty of humans to continue what God started. Second, human must create with the best that they have.

People have two options. They can live a life of passivity, thinking that as long as they do no wrong, they are pious and are fulfilling what God expects of them. As long as they wear religious clothing and decorate their dwellings with religious symbols, as long as they do not use improper language and mention God frequently in their conversation, they are doing what is proper. Such people fail to realize that they are acting like vegetating animals, like cows chewing contentedly on meadow grass, cows that do no wrong. There is no doubt that this was not what God intended. If this was God's desire, He would not have created humans, only cows.

The second option, one that is more difficult, is to live an active and creative life. Like the building of the Tabernacle, this requires the giving of our best, using our reasoning to improve ourselves and others, joining God and other people in making a better world.

Some call this duty *tikkun haolam*, "fixing up the world." This term is satisfactory as long as we realize that the world, created by God, needs no repair, but it does require maintenance and a need to continue what God started.

Summary

The story of the building of the Tabernacle is compared by parallel use of words and narratives to the creation of the world to teach two lessons. Creation was accomplished by God who fashioned a perfect world, but who made it clear by many means, including the Tabernacle story, that people need to continue the acts of creation. The Israelites are told to create the Tabernacle themselves; it was not produced miraculously by God. The Tabernacle serves as a symbol of all human activities. Just as the Tabernacle was only built when the people contributed the best they had, so people must use their intelligence and give their best abilities to continue God's creation and improve the world.

* * *

There is a Chassidic legend about the Seer of Lublin.

A distraught woman and her husband came to the rabbi for help. "We have been trying for years to have a child, but were not successful. We have come to you for your prayer."

"I will be happy to pray for you," said the rabbi, "if you give me half of what you earn in a year."

"Please rabbi, we can not afford so much money! We are poor people. As it is, we don't have enough to live on," said the husband. "Please help us without pay."

"The best I can do," said the rabbi, "is to pray for you for a quarter of your income."

The husband turned to his wife and said, "What choice do we have. Let's pay the rabbi what he demands so that we can have a child."

"We do have a choice," said the wife. "We can leave and pray on our own."

As the couple was leaving, the rabbi said, "This is what I wanted to teach you. Don't rely on others. Do things yourself."

The story ends with the announcement that the couple had a child within a year. Whether they did or not, what is certain is that after they left they had a sense of dignity.

Pekudei

The Jewish contribution to the study of history

Exodus 39:7 repeats the requirement of *Exodus* 28:29. The high priest Aaron was directed to wear eight garments, one of which was a breast plate with the names of the twelve sons of Jacob. He was instructed to wear it over his heart when he "enters the Sanctuary, as a constant remembrance (*zikaron*) before the Lord."

Questions:
1. Why should we remember?
2. What are the most important items that we should remember?
3. What contribution did Judaism make to the study of history?

Zechut Avot
The biblical commentator Ovadiah Sforno (born around 1470 and died about 1550) offered a problematical interpretation. He contended that the high priest wore the breastplate with the names of Jacob's sons so that God would see the names, remember the righteousness of the twelve ancestors and grant blessings to their offspring because of the "merits" of the ancestors.

There are two difficulties with this statement. The first is the outrageous, even sacrilegious notion that God forgets and needs reminders. However, this can be understood figuratively: it denotes that the Israelites (not God) have a duty to remember.

The second is that the curious concept of *zechut avot,* "ancestral merit." It is not accepted by all Jews. This is the belief that the merit of righteous ancestors can be stored up – like a bank deposit – and disbursed to unrighteous descendants when they need assistance.

It is true that the concept is found in the prayer service of the High Holidays and is repeated frequently in other Jewish documents. However, the Siddur, the daily prayer book, and the Machzor, the holiday prayer book, are the collective ideology of different kinds of Jews. They contain many ideas that some Jews accept literally and others only figuratively. A rationalist can interpret a statement such as "Remember for our benefit the good deeds of Abraham, Isaac and Jacob," figuratively. It advises people to remember their ancestors' good deeds and emulate them, and thereby bring blessings to their lives.

"Remembering" in Scripture

The concept of remembering is found frequently in the Bible. There are over two hundred times that a form of the verb *zakhor*, "remember," is mentioned in the Bible. The near synonyms *shamor* and *pakad*, the latter being the root of the name of this week's Torah portion, is found in the Torah in some form over four hundred and two hundred times, respectively. Sometimes it is God who is remembering. At other times, it is the Israelites who are obliged to remember.

Examples of God remembering include the following. In *Exodus* 3:16, God directs Moses to tell the elders of Israel, during their Egyptian enslavement, that "I have surely remembered you." In *Genesis* 9:15, *Leviticus* 26:4, *Psalms* 105:8 and other biblical verses God assures the people of Israel that He will remember His covenant with them forever. In *Jeremiah* 2:2, God informs the nation, "I will remember for you the affection of your youth." In *Genesis* 8:1, "God remembers Noah"; in 19:29 it is Abraham; in 30:22, it is Rachael.

God charged Israel to remember in verses such as: "Remember the days of old, consider the ages past" (*Deuteronomy* 32:7). "Remember His marvelous works that He has done, His wonders and the judgments of His mouth" (*I Chronicles* 16:12). "Remember these things, Jacob.... Never forget Me" (*Isaiah* 44:21). "Remember what Amalek did to you" (*Deuteronomy* 25:17). "Remember what Balak of Moab plotted against you" (*Micah* 6:5). "You must remember that you were slaves (*Deuteronomy* 5:15, 15:15, 16:12, 24:18, 22). "Remember the Lord your God" (*Deuteronomy* 8:18). "Remember what the Lord your God did to Pharaoh and to all Egypt" (*Deuteronomy* 7:18, 24:9). "Remember the Sabbath day" (*Exodus* 20:8), "the day you came out of Egypt" (*Exodus* 13:3), "how you made the Lord your God angry in the wilderness" (*Deuteronomy* 9:7), "what the

Lord did to Miriam" (*Deuteronomy* 24:9), "what Amalek did to you" (*Deuteronomy* 25:17), "His covenant forever" (*I Chronicles* 16:15).

A mystical approach

In the sixteenth century, the mystics maintained that a person should daily mention six of the commands to remember. The mystics apparently considered these six the most essential of the multitude of mandates to remember. The six are listed in most siddurs, "daily prayer books," at the end of the morning services, and some Jews recite them as the mystics encouraged them to do. These six are:

1. The exodus from Egypt
2. The Sabbath
3. The day you (your ancestors) stood at Horeb (Mount Sinai) to receive the Decalogue
4. How you angered God in the wilderness
5. What God did to Miriam
6. What Amalek did to you.

Remembering and history

The Greek historian Herodotus (about 484–425 B.C.E.) is generally called the "father of history." He wrote his famous history of the Greek wars, as he said, to preserve "from decay the remembrance of what men have done, and to preserve the great and wonderful actions of the Greeks and the barbarians [non-Greeks] from losing their due need of glory." Herodotus wrote in order that people should not forget. However, neither he nor the other early Greek historians attempted to draw moral principles and political insights from the past.

Judaism made this decisive contribution to civilization through the writings in the Bible. Scripture saw God's will and purpose in historical experiences, a divine challenge and a need for a proper human response.

While it is certainly true that the pagan gods appeared in the Greek myths and histories, and many Greeks memorized the tales, but the gods were seen, on the whole, as mischievous human-like beings, not instructors of moral conduct.

When the Jew, on the other hand, is enjoined to remember standing at Sinai, he is reminded of the purposes of the law, the sanctity of God and the relationship between humans and the divine. When the Jew is told to recall the exodus from Egypt, he is encouraged to elevate himself and others from all manners of slavery. When he is obliged to remember how his ancestors angered God, how Amalek attacked the Israelites, and how even Miriam, Moses' sister, acted improperly when she slandered her brother, he is taught to avoid such behavior. When he is instructed to keep the Sabbath in mind, he realizes, sometimes only unconsciously, that weekday work must be put into a perspective: work, indeed everything in life, must have an intellectual, moral and spiritual objective.

Summary

Rationalists must not rush to condemn every mystical notion. The idea of *zechut avot*, "ancestral merit" can be understood to encourage us to think about the good deeds of our ancestors and copy them. Similarly, the mystical practice of reading a list of six of the dozens of biblical commands to "remember" serves a lofty concept of history, an idea that the Jews introduced to the world. History is not, as Herodotus and other ancients imagined, a vehicle to assure that glorious events will not be forgotten. The Jewish contribution to historical writing is to recall events that encourage intellectual and moral growth. The Bible repeatedly insists that Jews remember so that their future will be improved.

Can we bewitch God with sacrifices, prayers and incantations?

The biblical book *Leviticus* describes elaborate ceremonies of sacrifices. Although the rabbis maintained that the sacrifices were accompanied by prayers, most people do not realize that prayer is not explicitly mentioned in the Pentateuch, the five books of Moses.

The first biblical person who is explicitly said to have prayed was a woman, Hannah the mother of Samuel, in the book of *I Samuel* 1 and 2. She prayed for the birth of a child. Her silent prayer surprised the pious high priest Eli. He thought that she was drunk.

Although the Pentateuch certainly describes many incidences of people speaking or calling to God, they are not specifically praying.

Questions
1. What was the ancient Greek Plato's and Galen's attitude to prayer?
2. What did Maimonides think about prayer?
3. What was Nachmanides view of prayer?
4. Do prayers work?

Plato
The title to this comment are words taken from the Greek philosopher Plato (427–347 B.C.E.) in his *Laws*. Despite being religiously-minded and mystical, he insisted that God has no need for sacrifices, prayers and incantations. God is "most wise and both willing and able to care [for the world]" without human help or reminders. Plato insisted that God is not like the Persian officials of his day who demanded bribes and who made decisions based on the size of these gifts.

In the *Alcibiades II*, a philosophical dialogue ascribed to Plato, but generally seen to be of much later origin, the philosopher tells an amusing story about prayers that meshes perfectly with the Platonic anti-elongated-prayer attitude.

He describes the Spartans, a Greek nation dwelling south of Plato's Athens, as a people who pray to their god with a brief statement. They request that he grant them whatever he considers to be good. After loosing many battles against Sparta, the Athenians petitioned their god to tell them why he refuses to grant their request for victory. "After all," they complained, "we give you so much: we heap on the sacrifices and pray at great length." Their god answered, "I would rather have the [Spartan] reverent reserve."

The author of *Alcibiades II* also writes: "It would be a strange thing if the gods had regard for our gifts and sacrifices instead of our souls, and the piety and justice that should be found in all of us."

Galen

The second century C.E. Greek physician Galen, the most influential doctor and medical educator that ever lived, was convinced that the only true way to worship God was with observation, reason and experimentation, not prayer and sacrifice. He wrote in his *De Usu Partium:*

> I consider that I am really showing him reverence, not when I offer him numerous [sacrifices]… but when I learn to know his wisdom, power and goodness, and then make them known to others.

Maimonides

Jews differ on the subject of prayer, as they do on many other subjects, since there is almost nothing in Judaism demanding a catechism of beliefs. Maimonides (1138–1204) and Nachmanides (1194–1270), for example, took opposite positions. And, there are other opinions on the subject.

Maimonides' view can be summarized briefly from his *Guide of the Perplexed.* It is found in sections such as 3:16, 32 and 46.

1. God is one and omnipotent. This means that God is all powerful. He is able to do whatever He desires. He needs absolutely nothing from anyone or anything.

2. God is omniscient. This means that He knows everything. There is nothing that a human can tell Him that He does not know.

3. God is good. Everything He does is good. There is no evil associated with God.

4. God created the world to function according to the laws of nature. There is no need to change these laws since God considered everything that will happen before he instituted them. The laws of nature are good.

5. While it is true that people suffer evil, evil does not come from God. There are three sources of evil: (1) Since all people are different from each other, no law, human or divine, can be created that will benefit everyone alike. In fact many laws that are extremely beneficial for most humans will be harmful to some people. Thus, the laws of nature are good for the world as a whole, but some people will be hurt by it. An example is hurricanes that benefit the earth but whose force can hurt and even kill people. (2) Evil can also come from other people, as when one individual hurts another. (3) One can also do evil to himself, as when he overeats or fails to do exercise.

Paying close attention to Maimonides' logic shows that his arguments are both logical and persuasive. Since God has no needs, He does not require sacrifices, prayer or incantations. Also, since He knows everything, He already considered whatever a human could think of and has already decided to do what is good. Additionally, since He knowingly created a world that functions according to the laws of nature in a manner that is good for the world, He has no need or intention of altering these laws, and no human attempt by prayer, sacrifice, magic or incantation will change anything.

According to this reasoning, any attempt to change matters by prayer, sacrifice, magic and incantations is arrogant. The person doing so is implying that God acted unwisely and in an evil fashion. It also implies that he, the human, is wiser than God and knows better than God how the world should be managed.

Maimonides supports his position with quotes from several prophets who spoke against sacrifices. He states that although God has absolutely no need for sacrifices and prayers, He allows humans to sacrifice and pray because people feel that they need them. These activities help many people feel closer to God.

Although Maimonides does not use these terms, he would probably agree that the benefit of sacrifices and prayers are suggested by the Hebrew words for these activities. The Hebrew for sacrifices is *karban*, which means drawing near: sacrifices and prayers, although of no use to God, help people feel that they are closer to God. The Hebrew for prayer is *tefillah*, from the root *pll*, which means "judging," for prayer and sacrifices could encourage people to judge themselves. They could use the activities as periods of self reflection.

Maimonides sees absolutely no value in magic and incantations. They are totally foolish and akin to idolatry. Nevertheless, as a physician who recognized the impact of the mind on the body, he allows foolish and ignorant sick people to use incantations when they are deathly sick and convinced that the incantation will help them get well.

Nachmanides

The mystic Nachmanides' reasoning and the result of his thinking is totally opposite that of his predecessor Maimonides. It can be summarized as follows:

1. God is one, yet He is composed of ten parts, each of which has a different function. God is not all-powerful because He needs humans to help Him align these parts properly and get them to function in the best fashion.

2. God knows everything, but can be persuaded to see things in a different way.

3. God is good, but the world is full of demons and other bad beings that need to be combated. A person can turn to God for help in overcoming these evil beings.

4. The world does not function according to the laws of nature. God is involved every moment in everything that happens in this world. No leaf, for example, falls unless God wills it to do so. Thus there are opportunities at every moment to persuade God to do something different than He may have intended.

Nachmanides was reluctant, for understandable reasons, to state his mystical views openly, so he merely hinted at them. We need to turn to his super commentator Rabbeinu Bachya ben Asher (died around 1310) and others for a clear understanding of what Nachmanides is saying. In his commentary to

Leviticus 1:9, Nachmanides mentions that the true purpose of sacrifices is explained by mysticism: "By way of the truth, there is a hidden secret in the offerings." God needs sacrifices for "the sake of *yichud*," to unify His various components. This is the meaning of *karban*, "bring near," to bring God's ten parts near, in proper order. Once humans do this, God functions properly and peace is brought to earth.

Many, if not most, people today accept the Nachmanidean stance that God needs or benefits from sacrifices and prayers without realizing that this idea is grounded in his notion of mysticism.

Zohar

Interestingly, the mystical book *Zohar* (1, 143b), which modern biblical scholars contend was composed around the end of the thirteenth century, about the time of Nachmanides death, maintains that humans should not expect that their prayers will be fulfilled. Commenting on the prayers/blessings that Isaac gave to his son Jacob, the *Zohar* admits that the prayer/blessings were never fulfilled. Isaac prayed/blessed Jacob in *Genesis* 27:37 that he would be the master of Esau his brother and that Jacob would be sustained with grain and wine. Jacob, the Zohar admits, never ruled over Esau. Furthermore, he was a shepherd and never worked as a farmer who harvested grain and wine.

Summary

Most people accept the concept of prayer and sacrifices as proper forms of worship. However, some ancient non-Jewish scholars questioned whether the practices affected God. Similarly, some Jewish scholars, such as Maimonides and the *Zohar*, admitted that people should not expect that their prayers will be fulfilled. Nevertheless, all agree that prayers can affect humans in one way: it can remind people to think about their lives and about God.

Tzav

The seven Noahide commandments[*]

The biblical portion called *Tzav*, "command," like many other biblical portions, reports God's decrees to the Israelites, the nation that would be called Jews from the beginning of the second Temple period (around 516 B.C.E.). The Talmud, *Makkoth* 23b states, "Rabbi Simlai [who lived in the second half of the third century C.E.] preached, 'six hundred and thirteen precepts were communicated to Moses'" as divine mandates for the Jewish people. In contrast, the talmudic rabbis taught that non-Jews were handed only seven injunctions, called the seven Noahide commandments.

Questions
1. What is the source of the seven Noahide commandments?
2. Where are they discussed in Rabbinic literature?
3. What are the seven edicts?
4. Why were there seven and not others?

The source
The Bible informs us that Noah's generation violated God's commands. The rabbis felt that although these rules were not recorded in the Torah, the people knew them before the era of Noah and passed them on to their children. But Noah's generation ignored them.

They were recorded for the first time around the year 200 C.E. in a work called the *Tosefta*. They were repeated in the twelfth century by Moses Maimonides (1138–1204) in his *Mishne Torah*, his code of Jewish law. Maimonides revised the order of the commands.

---

[*] Rabbi Menachem M. Schneerson, the Lubavitcher Rebbe, requested the author to write this article, and it appeared for the first time, in a slightly different version, in the Lubavitch magazine *Wellsprings*.

The *Tosefta* lists them as follows:
1. The requirement to establish law courts,
2. the prohibition against blasphemy,
3. idolatry,
4. sexual immorality,
5. bloodshed,
6. theft, and
7. the rule forbidding the eating of a limb torn from a living animal.

Maimonides ordered the commands differently:
1. the prohibition against idolatry,
2. blasphemy,
3. bloodshed,
4. sexual immorality,
5. theft,
6. the requirement to establish law courts, and
7. the rule forbidding the eating of a limb torn from a living animal.

Why are the lists ordered differently?

It seems that the *Tosefta*, which starts its list with law courts, focuses on humanity. It sees the laws as guides to make it possible for people to survive. Maimonides orders his list to help people improve.

Idolatry

Maimonides forbids idolatry first. This rule teaches people that they should not use religious symbols without trying to understand their divine purpose. It instructs them to focus their attention on God as the purpose and goal of every thought and action. They need to train themselves to fear, love and understand God, in that order. They must comprehend that since every human is created in God's image with a divine spark, they are obliged to fear, love and understand everyone. They are required to bring people together and combine their divine sparks in a blaze that emits light and warmth to all. This, according to Maimonides, is a first principle.

Rabbi Schneur Zalman, the first Lubavitch Rebbe, demonstrated the significance of this teaching daily. Once, for example, when he was occupying an apartment above his son and infant grandchild, he heard his grandchild crying. He left his studies and descended to his son's apartment where he saw the child in one corner and the child's father in another absorbed in Torah study. He lifted and soothed the child, and said to his son: "All of our study has no effect as long as we don't hear a child's cry."

It may be that it was this teaching of his father that made it possible for his son to become the second Lubavitcher Rebbe.

Blasphemy

The second Noahide command prohibits blasphemy. Cursing God is a radical negation of the divine. It rejects the importance of God. In a positive sense, it directs us to live a life that highlights the existence and importance of God for others.

The Talmud tells us that Shimon ben Shetach lived such a life. He once sent his disciples to buy him a saddle. They returned overjoyed. They found a diamond in the saddle. They praised their teacher for being blessed by God because under the strict rule of law, the seller, having completed the sale, had sold him both the saddle and its contents. But, Shimon ben Shetach told his students to return the diamond.

When the seller retrieved the jewel, he exclaimed: "Blessed is the God of Shimon ben Shetach!"

Shimon ben Shetach's behavior is better than any sermon. It prompts praise of God and, more importantly, a realization that God's ways are beneficial and right.

Murder

The third command prevents murder. Those who train their thought on humans stress that this rule minimizes strife and preserves civilization. This is true. However, those who are God-oriented recognize that it does more. It requires that we never extinguish, or even mar, the spark of God in people – even though we have not killed them. We must always recall that every human carries the divine spark, and we therefore dare not do to humans what we would not do to God. Just as we must not strike out against God with words, so we must never belittle another human with our words: we may not say anything derogatory to or about another human being, for this is tantamount to murder.

Sexual relations

The fourth command regulates sexual relations, incest, adultery and bestiality. Maimonides taught us in his *Guide of the Perplexed* and other books that all of life requires control: habits of action performed according to the golden mean. This Noahide rule controls the misdirection of thought and behavior. It encourages people to maximize rationality. It also motivates the strengthening of bonds of kinship.

Theft

Theft seems to be a simple and obvious command. Why is it included among the Noahide commands? The same question can be asked about murder.

The seven Noahide rules are found in many indirect statements in the early Bible chapters. The commands suggest more inclusive and more significant values than would be apparent at first glance. *Genesis* 2:16, for example, is one source for the Noahide interdiction against theft: "You may eat of every tree of the garden except from the tree of good and evil." This verse informs us much more than a mere prohibition against theft. It teaches that everything belongs to God. We steal from God when we take anything from another.

Law courts

The Maimonidean sixth command is the *Tosefta's* first. From the perspective of human behavior, laws begin the ordering of society. From a moral standpoint, however, Maimonides' changed order of the commands imparts much more: society starts with a value system recognizing God. The requirement for laws comes sixth in the latter system and directs the development of a program that assures the observance of the remaining six commands. This order also teaches that religious ceremonies and practices, like laws generally, are needed as reminders that give direction, milestones and goals.

Eating a limb torn from a living animal

We have seen that Moses Maimonides made an orderly presentation of rules that improves humanity. The Noahide commands, according to Maimonides' order, educate us first about God as the source, foundation and goal of every thought and action. The second induces behavior that motivates others to praise God. The third helps people see the sparks, or elements, of God in all people and make them realize their responsibilities toward all of humanity. The fourth teaches restraint in thought, speech and action. The fifth reminds people that everything belongs to God and encourages thinking about the consequences of this understanding. The sixth establishes a program of reminders to preserve the values and promote proper behavior. Why does society need the seventh from *Genesis* 9:4, "Surely flesh with its life blood you shall not eat"? Logically, we would have expected the final statement to be the highest principle.

Actually it is. It teaches the most difficult lesson. We must go beyond relating to the divine in humans. The seventh command mandates respect for animal and inanimate objects. It requires people to behave properly with everything in an ever-ascending movement toward God.

We cannot ascend the ladder of progress unless we descend, as the first Lubavitcher Rebbe, to assure that nothing, absolutely nothing, is in pain. We must step carefully, making sure that even stones under our feet do not protest, "How dare you walk on me without observing the wishes of God."

People-oriented laws maintain human existence. They secure peace of mind and protect the status quo. Theocentric laws, the order of Maimonides, do more. They distinguish the desirable from the undesirable, bring real happiness to body and soul, and lead to perfection.

Summary

It is not surprising that Maimonides' Code sets the Noahide commandments just before the discussion of the messianic age. The Noahide rules set out a guide toward the best in life. Properly understood and fully observed they can lead humanity into the messianic age.

A story highlights the goal of these commands.

A youngster was waiting at the seashore for a ship to take him home. An adult stopped by, mocked him and said he was standing in the wrong place. He suggested that the boy walk three miles to the regularly-established passenger pick-up area. The youngster stood his ground. Shortly thereafter, the boat came downstream. It turned toward him, and released its plank to take him aboard. The adult looked in surprise. "How did you know," he asked, "that the ship would stop to pick you up?" "Simple," replied the boy. "You see, the captain is my father."

Once we realize that God is the parent and captain of all, and act accordingly, life receives greater meaning and direction, and God takes us home. This is the ultimate goal of the seven Noahide commandments.

Shemini

Why keep kosher?

The eleventh chapter of *Leviticus* specifies some, but not all, of the basic kosher laws, which were later explained and elaborated upon by the rabbis in the Oral Law. The physical characteristics of animals – split hoofs and bringing up its cud – classify those that can be eaten. Similarly, fish that possess fins and scales can be consumed. The eatable birds and teeming creatures are identified by name.

Questions
1. How do the above-mentioned three commands blend with the other Torah food regulations?
2. What are some of the reasons for these laws?
3. Does *Leviticus* 11 reveal reasons for the commands?

Torah food laws
An understanding of the rationale underlying the kosher rules requires one to grasp at least three things:

1. The commands prohibiting certain animals, birds and fish are only a small part of many biblical food prohibitions. Each ban has its own reason. Among others, Jews are barred by biblical and Rabbinic enactments from eating blood, a kid seethed in its mother's milk, mixed meat and milk foods, the sciatic nerve, certain animal fats, animals that died a natural death, unsalted animals, animals that were not slaughtered, mixed species, consuming *terumah* and *maser* by an Israelite, eating the edge of one's field and the growth of trees in its early years.

2. In addition to realizing that the food laws are quite extensive, one should also know that the practice of calling only certain food restrictions "unkosher" is not biblical. The term "kosher" does not appear in the

Pentateuch. It is found only three times in post-Pentateuchal scriptural books – *Esther* 8:5 and *Ecclesiastes* 10:10 and 11:6 – and none of these three sources use the term "kosher" to refer to food laws. The term "kosher" or "kashrut," as it is used today, means "fit" or "proper." There is no indication as to what "fit" applies. It may refer to fitness for life, holiness, or to something else, such as the Tabernacle worship. The Bible gives no reason for its commands about animals, birds and fish.

3. It should also be understood that *Leviticus* 11, which mentions the ban on eating certain animals, birds and fish, is part of a larger priestly code of purity, for the majority of the chapter prohibits contamination and contact with the dead bodies of the prohibited animals. The dietary laws are repeated in *Deuteronomy* 14, but *Deuteronomy* does not recap the laws of contamination. *Leviticus* 11 ends the dietary and contamination laws by stating that avoidance of contamination is a prerequisite to becoming a holy people: "For I am the Lord who brought you up from the land of Egypt to be your God – you must be holy, for I am holy." *Exodus* 22:30 also mentions holiness as a reason for avoiding contaminated items.

In short, what we call today the laws of "kashrut" is only a small part of the Torah food prohibitions, the Bible itself never separated one segment of the food laws (the rules of "kashrut") from the others, and even the laws of permitted animals, birds and fish are mixed with rules concerning contaminated foods/animals.

Ignoring the other food rules, why were certain animals, birds and fish prohibited?

Nachmanides

The Spanish mystic Nachmanides (1195–1270) focused on the fact that these dietary decrees are joined to the laws of purity in the biblical section concerning the Tabernacle, and he equates the two. In the beginning of his comment on chapter 11, he wrote that the purpose of both laws is to protect the sanctity of the Tabernacle. He states that both sets of commands apply to the Israelites and the priests, "but the subject matter of the section affects the priests more than the Israelites because they need to guard themselves from touching impure objects, since they must enter the Sanctuary and they eat hallowed foods" which are prohibited to be eaten when the priests are impure. The

Israelites are "also warned against eating impure foods, so that they would not defile the Tabernacle and its hallowed objects."

(Curiously, in his comment on 11:9, he explains that fish without fins and scales are banned for health reasons, because they swim in the deepest cold and muddy waters. He does not assign a health reason for the prohibited animals and birds, and the health rationale seems to conflict with the idea of sanctity that he mentioned earlier.)

Moses Isserles

The Polish expert on *Halakhah*, Moses Isserles, better known as "the Rema," (1525 or 1530–1572) concentrated on the chapter's final statement about holiness, and insisted that the holiness rationale, mentioned for contaminated substances, also applies to the dietary injunctions. In his comment on the *Shulchan Aruch, Yoreh Deah* 81:7, he contended that consuming non-kosher food deadens one's spiritual capacity to the extent that one does not even realize the loss. He advises that even though most laws do not apply to young children, one must protect small children from this spiritual loss and not allow them to eat non-kosher foods.

Tobit

The ancient apocryphal book *Tobit* – of unknown date, but perhaps as early as 550 B.C.E. – which was not included in the Bible, also apparently concentrated its attention on the holiness aspect that is mentioned in the chapter. Since the basic meaning of *kodesh*, "holiness," intends "separation," the book states that the food laws are designed to keep Jews apart from non-Jews.

Letter of Aristeas, Philo, *Genesis Rabbah* and *Leviticus Rabbah*

Holiness can also denote a proper life. Thus it is no surprise that the first century B.C.E. volume *Letter of Aristeas* suggests that the food laws teach Jews about justice and other moral lessons. Similarly, the philosopher Philo (20 B.C.E.–50 C.E.) wrote that creatures with evil instincts are forbidden because their instincts can be transmitted to humans who eat them. The Midrashim *Genesis Rabbah* 44:1 and *Leviticus Rabbah* 13:3 (around the fourth century C.E.) are similar when they state that the laws refine people.

Rashi

The Bible and Talmud commentator Rashi (1040–1105) relied on the *Midrash Tanchuma* and drew his reason for the dietary laws from a single word. He insisted that non-kosher foods kill people. This, he states, is evident by the Torah's use of the introductory words "these are the living things." The phrase, according to him, does not refer to the living things that may be eaten, but to those animal foods that sustain life; while unkosher animals/foods do the opposite – kill. Neither the Midrash nor Rashi explain what kind of life they mean. Are they talking about health, spiritual life, intelligence, life after death, or something else?

Mystics

Some mystics seem to have answered the question we asked about the Midrash and Rashi. Joseph Gikatilla (end of the 10th century), Menahem Recanati (about the beginning of the 14th century) and Isaac Arama (c. 1460–1545), for example, insisted that improper food can defile the body, pollute the soul and confuse the intellect.

Maimonides

The Nagid (the spiritual and political Jewish Egyptian leader) Maimonides (1138–1204) presents his reasons for the scriptural commandments in chapters 25–54, the final chapters of his *Guide of the Perplexed*. His general explanations of the biblical commands include three things: instilling proper ideas, improving society and improving the individual. He writes in chapter 31 that the purpose of "every one of the 613 precepts serves to inculcate some truth, to remove some erroneous opinion, to establish proper relations in society, to diminish evil, to train in good manners, or to warn about bad habits. All this depends on three things: opinions, morals [individual behavior], and social conduct" (translation by M. Friedlander).

Maimonides sees a health advantage to the individual in the laws of kashrut, specifically that "the food that is forbidden [is forbidden] by the law [because it] is unwholesome."

Ibn Ezra and the *Sifra*

The Spanish Jewish Bible commentator Abraham ibn Ezra (1089–1164) and the *Midrash Sifra* (fourth century C.E.) of the Land of Israel focus on the fact that the Bible offers no reason for the food commandments, and emphasize that they are divine decrees. Ibn Ezra simply states that we can not know the reason. *Sifra* warns the Jew, "Do not say, 'I do not like pig's flesh.' Instead, say, 'I like it but I must abstain because the Torah forbids it.'"

Summary

The biblical food laws are quite extensive and include many prohibitions beyond the commonly recognized rules banning the eating of certain animals, bird and fish. The term "kosher" is not biblical, and was selected in post-biblical times to include some of these forbidden food rules. Each of the banned foods have there own rationale.

The prohibitions against eating certain animals, birds and fish are detailed in *Leviticus* 11 and *Deuteronomy* 14, where they are combined with bans against certain contaminated animals/foods, such as the carcasses of prohibited animals. The Bible gives no reason for the food restrictions in these chapters.

The ancient sources and Bible commentators offered a host of widely disparate grounds for these commands. The rationales varied according to where the analyst focused his attention. Some looked at the juxtaposition of the food laws with those concerning contamination. Others took the purpose of the contamination directives – holiness – and applied it the food decree. Several drew their interpretation from their understanding of a single word, even taken out of context. Another group, like Maimonides, relied on their general view of the aim of the divine commands – in Maimonides' case, they were promulgated for health or ethical reasons. Still others, such as ibn Ezra and the *Midrash Sifra,* insist that Jews observe kashrut because God told them to do so, and for no other reason.

In short, the rationales offered for the biblical dietary regulations illustrate the many and divergent concerns of Jewish commentators.

Tazria

An introduction to haphtarot and Don Isaac Abravanel

The Shabbat and holiday Torah reading service is followed by a recitation from one of the books of the prophets and is called the haphtarah, or haphtarot in the plural. The name means "conclusion," and is so called because it follows and ends the Torah service. The Hebrew Bible is called *Tanach*, which is an acronym for the three parts of the Bible: Torah (the five books of Moses), *Neviim* (the Prophets) and *Ketuvim* (the Writings, such as the book of Psalms). The haphtarot are selections from the middle group.

The earliest report of the practice of reading from the Prophets on the Sabbath in the Synagogue is found in the first century New Testament book Luke 4:17–20. The first mention that such a portion was read after the Torah reading is in the second century Mishna, *Megillah* 4:1. However, we no longer know when the practice of the prophetical recital actually began.

Many scholars believe that the custom started in the second century B.C.E., during the Maccabean period when the Jews were forbidden by the Syrian-Greek king to read the Torah in the Synagogue. The Jews circumvented the decree somewhat by reading a selection from the Prophets that corresponded in some way with the contents of the Torah portion. This reminded the people of their long-standing tradition to read the Torah in the Synagogue on the Shabbat and holidays as well as the contents of that Shabbat's portion. Thus, for example, the portion of *Tazria* deals with the laws of leprosy, so a story from *II Kings* 4:42–5:19 was selected since it tells the story of the leper Naaman.

When the Maccabees defeated the Syrian-Greeks and Torah reading was restored to the Synagogue, it is believed that the people decided to continue the new tradition of reading the haphtarot; however they placed the reading after the more significant Torah portion.

Questions

1. What is the story of Naaman, the haphtarah of *Tazria?*
2. How is the story interpreted by Don Isaac Abravanel?
3. Who was Abravanel?
4. How does Abravanel explain:

> a. Why did Naaman merit that "through him the Lord gave victory"?
>
> b. Why did Naaman bring so many gifts with him to the prophet Elisha?
>
> c. What made Naaman feel insulted?
>
> d. Why did Elisha tell Naaman to duck seven times in the Jordan?
>
> e. What prompted Naaman to want to take Israeli earth with him to Aram?
>
> f. Why did Elisha refuse to accept the gift that Naaman offered him?

The story of Naaman in the haphtarah

Naaman was a general of the army of the king of Aram. The Bible reports that God gave Aram victory through him. He was well-liked by the king and very successful, but he was a leper.

Naaman captured a young Israelite girl who told him that there was a prophet in Samaria (Israel) who could cure him of his leprosy. Naaman passed on this information to the king of Aram, who sent a letter to the king of Israel. The letter said that he was sending Naaman to the king of Israel "that you should heal him of his leprosy." The letter had no mention of the prophet. Naaman went to Israel with many gifts of silver, gold and clothing for the prophet. When the king of Israel received the letter, he thought that the king of Aram was seeking a pretext to attack his kingdom again. He knew that he had no power to heal anyone.

The prophet Elisha sent a message to the king of Israel that he could cure Naaman, and Naaman was sent to him. Naaman came to the prophet's house, but the prophet did not go out to greet him. Instead, he sent a servant to tell Naaman that he should bathe in the Jordan seven times and he would be cured. Naaman was enraged and left, but his servants suggested that he comply with the prophet's instructions. He did so and was cured.

He returned to Elisha and told him that he now knew that the God of Israel is the only God. He offered Elisha the huge gifts that he brought with him, but the prophet refused them. Naaman asked permission to take two mule loads of Israeli dirt back to Aram. Elisha told him to "go in peace."

Who is Don Isaac Abravanel?

Don Isaac Abravanel (1437–1508) was a wealthy statesman who worked for several non-Jewish governments, a bible commentator and non-rational philosopher. He was born in Portugal and successfully served in several different government positions, including being the treasurer to the king. In 1483, he was suspected of being part of a conspiracy against a new king and had to escape to save his life. He settled in Spain with much of his wealth. Within a year, he took a government position under Ferdinand and Isabella of Castile.

He was expelled from Spain with the other Jews in 1492 and went to Naples. Again, within a year, he assumed a position with the king of Naples. Various difficulties occurred in this country, so he left and he finally settled in Venice where he also undertook governmental activities.

He wrote quite a few works on Jewish subjects, including commentaries on the Pentateuch, the Prophets, the *Haggadah*, and *Pirke Avot*, as well as books designed to convince Jews that the Messiah would appear in 1503. His general practice was to introduce his Bible commentaries with a list of questions, which he followed with lengthy answers.

He also wrote several volumes in which he expressed his strong disagreement with the rational philosophy of Moses Maimonides. He opposed extreme rationalism and allegory because he was convinced that they were wrong and because he feared that a rational approach would undermine the faith of simple unknowledgeable Jews. He contended that the Torah should be viewed as the word of God that strengthens the bond between humans and the divine.

Abravanel rejected the Maimonidean views of miracles, prophecy, providence, angels, demons and, in general, how God functions. He argued that the world does not operate according to the laws of nature: all that occurs in this world is directly attributable to God who makes decisions on everything every moment. Prophecy is not a natural higher level of human intelligence, as Maimonides suggests, but the miraculous communication of truth from God to the righteous prophet. Angels and demons are not metaphoric expressions of natural forces, but actual existing beings that are involved in human lives. Midrashim are not invented stories designed to teach moral lessons or other truths, but they frequently record actual events. The Messianic Age is not a natural period of peace, but the coming of a miraculous Messiah who would rule over people of all nations and who would live during the time of the resurrection of the dead.

These anti-Maimonidean beliefs affected his interpretations of the biblical accounts, and are strikingly evident in his commentary on the Naaman story.

Abravanel's interpretation of the haphtarah

The aid that the prophet Elisha gave to Naaman, according to Abravanel, was Elisha's tenth miracle. Naaman was a very successful general of Aram because God had rewarded him, as the *Midrash* to *Psalms* 78 asserts, Naaman killed the evil Israelite king Ahab. Naaman and his king believed that the prophet Elisha had the miraculous power to cure him of his leprosy, but the king of Israel did not believe this.

When the Israelite king received the king of Aram's message, he understood that Aram wanted the king himself to perform some kind of miracle. He knew that he lacked the power to do so, and feared that Aram was using this matter as a pretext to attack Israel again. When Elisha heard what had happened, he suggested that the king send Naaman to him for he had the power to create miracles and his performance of a miracle would bring glory to God.

Naaman traveled to Israel with a large force and carried many gifts to impress the prophet. Elisha did not go out personally to greet the general because he wanted to make it clear that it was God and not he who would cure Naaman. Naaman did not know why Elisha seemingly ignored and insulted him. He expected that the prophet would stage some elaborate magic act, such as waving his hand over him while reciting mystical formula. Besides, he fumed, if water was a cure, there were two large rivers in Aram that he could use. They were bigger than the Jordan to which he was being summarily sent. So he felt degraded and decided to leave. However, his retainers appeased him and persuaded him to try Elisha's treatment.

Abravanel does not inform us why Elisha wanted him to duck in the Jordan seven times. Perhaps it was because the number seven was a significant spiritual number in both the Israel and Aram cultures, and would make an impression. In any event, the dunking was successful and Naaman returned to the prophet. He finally understood that his healing came from the God of Israel. The general offered the prophet the many gifts that he brought for him, but the prophet refused. This was another demonstration by Elisha that it was God, not he, who is involved in all that occurs on earth and who restored Naaman to health.

Naaman was so impressed that he decided that he wanted to worship God by bringing sacrifices to him even in his own country. He believed that a proper altar for God should be built from the earth of the land of Israel. He, therefore, requested earth of Israel from the prophet.

Summary

The practice of reading a portion from the prophets following the Torah reading is generally believed to have started before the Common Era during a period of persecution when the reading of the Torah was forbidden by Israel's enemy. The Jews decided to read a selection from the prophets that corresponded in some way with the forbidden Torah reading (and on special festivals to correspond to the occasion) so as to remember what Torah portion was scheduled to be read at that time. In *Tazria,* the Torah section mentions lepers and so does the haphtarah.

The haphtarah raises many questions. One of the commentators on the *Tanach* was Don Isaac Abravanel, a non-rationalist. His explanations of Scripture are generally interesting even to those who do not accept his premises. Among other things, Abravanel, like Yehudah Halevi, Nachmanides and many others, believed that God is involved daily in all earthly affairs, there are daily miracles, prophets receive messages directly from God in a supernatural way, and the truth about certain matters can be found in midrashic stories. He used these beliefs to explain the unusual story of Naaman and Elisha in the haphtarah.

Miriam: Some thoughts on a happy life

Leviticus 12–14 reveals the laws of the *mestzora,* a disease that the sages in the Babylonian Talmud, *Arachin* 15b and other sources, disclose was caused by slander. A case in point is the punishment of Moses' sister Miriam, for she slandered Moses.

Miriam is not mentioned frequently in Scripture. Her death is announced in *Numbers* 20:1. Her name occurs in two other Pentateuchal narratives: in *Exodus* 15 where she and other women sing to celebrate the Israelite deliverance from their erst-while taskmasters, the Egyptians, and in *Numbers* 12 when she criticizes her brother Moses' behavior to his wife and is summarily and severely punished. She is also refered to in *Exodus* 2 where she saves Moses from being killed with other Israelite males as Pharaoh had commanded. She is described there as Moses' sister, without being named. She is recalled briefly in two other verses. In *Numbers* 26:59, she is included in the list of children of Amram and Yocheved. In *Deuteronomy* 24:9, the final recollection, her punishment for her judgment of Moses is recalled and the Israelites are warned not to follow her behavior.

Of the three narratives about Miriam, the two earlier ones – saving her brother and her song of praise – are positive recollections. The third and final one – about her criticism of Moses' behavior – is conspicuously negative. Of the two simple statements, the one about her genealogy is neutral, without any judgment, but the reminiscence of her criticism, the last time that she is mentioned in the Torah, is a statement of disapproval.

Questions:
1. Can we say that the portrayal of Miriam is overall positive?
2. Is it significant that the final episode of her life is negative?
3. Did Miriam have a happy and successful life?

Pirke Avot on happiness and success:

The first century sage Hillel advises in *Pirke Avot* 2:3: "Do not be sure of yourself until the day of your death." This maxim may refer to a change in one's belief or an alteration in the circumstances of one's life

Some commentators think that Hillel's statement was prompted by an historical recollection. He may have recalled his former colleague Menahem. According to the Jerusalem Talmud, *Haggigah* 77b, "he [Menahem] went forth" and was succeeded by Shammai. One interpretation of "he went forth" is that he became a heretic of some kind. Similarly, Don Isaac Abravanel cites the Babylonian Talmud, *Berachot* 29a. The Talmud relates that John, the Hasmonean high priest who lived a century before Hillel, served in his office for eighty years, but at the end of his life he abandoned the ways of the Pharisees and became a Sadducee.

The fifteenth century philosopher Shem Tov ibn Shem Tov took a different approach. He saw Hillel commenting on the turning wheel of fortune. One day one is rich, the next poor; one day successful and happy, the next a failure and sad.

The latter interpretation may be apropos to Miriam.

Aristotle and Plutarch:

The fourth century B.C.E. Greek philosopher Aristotle, in his *Constitution of Athens*, and the second century C.E. Greek historian Plutarch in his *Parallel Lives*, as well as other ancients, recount the story of the sixth century B.C.E. Greek law giver Solon. After enacting laws for Athens, Solon visited the enormously rich king Croesus. Croesus was extremely proud of his fortune, but wanted to increase it by fighting the Persians and appropriating their wealth.

Croesus was a man who enjoyed his riches better when it was admired by someone of lesser wealth. Recognizing Solon as a brilliant scholar, he asked him if he had ever seen a happier man than he. Solon replied that he had. He told Croesus of Tellus who ended his life an honest and reputable man. Croesus was surprised and asked Solon if he knew anyone else. Solon said he also knew of two brothers who were very affectionate to their mother. Once when they saw that the oxen pulling their mother's cart were unable to move forward, they took the yoke on their own shoulders and brought their mother to her destination, where everyone marveled and called her a fortunate and happy mother. The brothers laid down to rest and died a painless and tranquil death from their exhaustion, amidst many honors.

Croesus did not understand that Solon was telling him that a person can not be called happy until after death. Croesus serves as a good example. Although he was one of the richest men of his generation, he died a terrible death. He lost his battle to the Persians and became their slave.

Evaluating Miriam's life:
There are two ways to view Miriam's life.

1. Happy:

Although there is little textual support other than the proximity of verses, the Babylonian Talmud, *Taanit* 9a, states that a well was given to the Israelites during their wilderness sojourn because of the "merit of Miriam." "When Miriam died the well disappeared, as it said [in *Numbers* 20:1], 'And Miriam died there,' and immediately following [in the next verse], 'And there was no water for the congregation.'" The Talmud is praising Miriam by stating that she had "merit" and by telling us that God performed a miracle for the Israelites on her behalf.

The Babylonian Talmud, *Bava Batra* 17a, relates, again with no textual support, that Miriam died like her brothers with the tranquil death of a "kiss of the Lord." The notion is based on the use of the words *al pi*, which is an idiom for "through," but which literally means "by the mouth." It is used for Moses in *Deuteronomy* 34:5 and for Aaron in *Numbers* 33:38. The words are not found to be associated with Miriam at all.

Clearly, the rabbis were seeking to show that Miriam ended her life meritoriously, despite the final explicit biblical verses that criticize her.

2. Unhappy:

There is also no certain basis for the opposite view, that Miriam died unhappy. However, there are some indications that this was the fact. First, as we noted, Jewish and non-Jewish sources suggest that the proper way of evaluating a life is to see how it ends. There is no doubt that Miriam acted bravely and properly in the first two episodes – watching out for Moses and singing praise to God. However, the final act that the Bible records is her criticism of her brother.

Scripture relates that God was not at all pleased with her behavior. It was only because of Moses' prayer that she was saved. Nevertheless, God punished her with leprosy for her act. This negative judgment is repeated in the final statement about her, that the Israelites should always remember why and how she was punished.

Second, rather than proving her merit, the two previously-mentioned talmudic statements may be seen as proof of her unhappy situation. Since both statements have little textual support, they may arguably persuade the opposite of what they intend.

The juxtaposition of Miriam's death and the story of the absence of water can be seen in an entirely different light: The verses were placed together to highlight that the Israelites did not weep for Miriam as they did at the death of her brothers. In fact, if they wept at that time, it was not for her, but for the loss of water.

Summary

Scripture does not explicitly evaluate whether Miriam ended her life well or not. If we seek to decide upon this matter, our decision can be only conjecture. The Talmud clearly extols her, but does so with no clear biblical support. She is said to have had a miracle performed because of her merit until the day of her death, and that God granted her the same tranquil end that He gave to her brothers. Yet, on the other hand, the Bible itself records an explicit prominent derogatory episode as her last appearance in Scripture. If she is evaluated based on her final act, she did not live successfully. If this interpretation is correct, it highlights Hillel's maxim, "Do not be sure of yourself until the day of your death" and do not rely on prior good deeds.

Pseudo-Jonathan, the Karaites and Yom Kippur

One of the Bible commentaries worthy of consideration and study is the translation/commentary called *Targum Pseudo-Jonathan*.

Questions
1. What is a *Targum?*
2. What is *Targum Pseudo-Jonathan?*

Targum

The noun *Targum* means "translation." It usually refers to a rendering from the biblical Hebrew into Aramaic, the *lingua franca*, the language spoken by most Jewish people until around 1000 C.E. There are three complete Jewish *Targums* on the five books of Moses, and quite a few fragmented versions, but *Pseudo-Jonathan* is unique. It has considerably more midrashic elaborations than any other *Targum,* and many of them are only found in this source. These elaborations make it more interesting than the better-known and rabbinically sanctioned *Targum Onkelos* and the newly discovered *Targum Neophyti. Targum Onkelos* has lately been shown to have been composed around 400 C.E. The scholars still differ as to when *Targum Neophyti* was written; some date it before and some after *Onkelos.*

Targum Pseudo-Jonathan

Pseudo-Jonathan is first mentioned in a book by an Italian Kabbalist in the fourteenth century of the Common Era. Most scholars recognize that the work was originally entitled *Targum Yerushalmi,* "Jerusalem Targum." The current name is the result of an historical happenstance: some scribe misinterpreted the abbreviation *TY,* which was the title of the translation, as *Targum Jonathan* (Hebrew, *Yonatan*). The scribe placed *Targum Jonathan* in place of the initials *TY.* This Jonathan was identified as Jonathan ben Uzziel, whom the Talmud names as the translator of the biblical books of the Prophets into Aramaic. Since this second century sage did not compose this *Targum,* scholars customarily call it *Pseudo-Jonathan* to note that it is a fiction to suppose that it is from the pen of Jonathan ben Uzziel.

It is generally understood today that the *Pseudo-Jonathan* translator borrowed his basic translation of the biblical words from the earlier *Targum Onkelos* and expanded it with midrashic elaborations from midrashic works, including some that are no longer extant, as well as some that its author may have invented.

Halakhic, that is, legal material in the *Targum*

Pseudo-Jonathan also contains a wealth of *halakhic* material; that is, statements that the translator believed are proper Jewish law. However, it is significant that over one hundred of these laws run counter to currently-accepted *halakhah*. This created problems for many scholars and resulted in a plethora of theories and books.

Unfortunately, these scholars failed to recognize that Rabbinic commentators, including the famous rabbinically-accepted Rashi, differentiated between the plain meaning of the biblical text and the *halakhic* interpretation that the rabbis derived from the text. The *halakhic* teachings may differ radically from the plain meaning of the words and were even sometimes opposite to what the text plainly states.

A classical example of this phenomenon is the passage that requires a criminal who tore out the eye of another to pay "an eye for an eye." This plainly means that the offender's eye is removed. However, the rabbis understood the verse to mean that the culprit pays monetary damages.

Unfortunately, as we stated, many Bible scholars do not know that rabbinically-recognized commentaries contain non-*halakhic* material. As a result there is a wealth of erroneous studies that attempt to explain why the author of *Pseudo-Jonathan* made statements that contradict established *halakhah*. One scholar, for example, insisted that the translator would "certainly" include only *halakhah* if he knew it. He explained the deviations from *halakhah* with "five rules." The last of the five was that when the translator was faced with a rabbinical dispute regarding the *halakhah*, he selected an opinion that he liked, based on no other principle but that he thought this must be the correct opinion. Frequently, said the scholar, the translator was wrong.

Dating *Targum Pseudo-Jonathan*

There is a widespread difference among *Targum* scholars as to the date of the composition of *Targum Pseudo-Jonathan*. They range from the time of Ezra, in the fifth century B.C.E., to the period of the Crusades, a span of 1500 years. However, the current conception dates it to just after the Arab conquest of the Middle East, around the ninth century.

Bernard Revel in the 1920's felt that *Pseudo-Jonathan* was composed around the ninth century to counteract the sectarian beliefs of the Karaites, a group that started around this time. The Karaites, like the Sadducees of the Second Temple period, rejected the idea of an Oral Torah and the traditions of the rabbis. They insisted that only the plain meaning of the Pentateuch, the five books of Moses, was binding law. Revel's view that this was the sole purpose of this *Targum* is rejected today, but it contains some truth. This is the obvious reason for some of the *Targum's* statements.

An example of a *Pseudo-Jonathan* interpretation

Leviticus 16:29 mandates that you must "afflict yourselves" (*t'anu et nafshotechem*). The Babylonian Talmud, *Yoma* 74b, interprets these words to mean that one is required to abstain from food and drink on the fast day of Yom Kippur. The Talmud adds that our practice is to abstain on Yom Kippur from four additional pleasures: the enjoyment of baths, anointing, shoes and sex.

Pseudo-Jonathan mentions that all five abstentions on Yom Kippur are biblically required. This is contrary to the rabbinical *halakhah* that only the abstention of food and drink is biblical. Revel notes that the sectarian Karaites insisted that Scripture only forbids food and drink, and since in their view the rabbinical additions are not binding and should be ignored, Jews would be permitted to bathe, anoint themselves, wear shoes and engage in marital intercourse on Yom Kippur. In order to contest this view and encourage the observance of the law as taught by the rabbis, Revel believed that the translator stated that the abstention from all five acts was biblical.

Summary

One of the sources for ancient biblical interpretations is the early scriptural translations. One set of translations is the rendering of the biblical Hebrew into Aramaic, the language spoken by Jews and other nations at the time of the composition of the translation. There are three complete Jewish versions, called *Targum*, a word meaning "translation." One of the three is known today as *Targum Pseudo-Jonathan*, and is so-called because Jonathan was not its author. This *Targum* contains more imaginative elaborations than the others. Like virtually all translations and commentaries, this *Targum* contains material that is contrary to accepted *halakhah*. An example is the *Targum's* statement that all five abstentions on Yom Kippur are of biblical origin. One scholar suggested that the *Targum* made this claim to counter the practice of the sectarian Karaites who eschewed rabbinical laws and insisted on observing only those laws defined in the Bible.

Kedoshim

Can one love another as one's self?

The well-known requirement of *Leviticus* 19:18 – "Love thy neighbor as yourself" – is difficult to understand and impossible to implement. The divine command has three words in Hebrew *v'ahavta lereiacha kamocha*. Each is hard to comprehend. A similar mandate is repeated in 19:34, regarding strangers that settle in land, *v'ahavta lo kamocha*, "Love him as yourself."

Questions
1. How significant is the command to love another as one's self?
2. What is difficult about the command?
3. What are some of the more significant views concerning its meaning?

Significance
The *Leviticus* 19:18 command has been deemed a fundamental divine decree since ancient times. The *Midrash Sifra* to this verse reports that Rabbi Akiva in the early second century of the Common Era identified it as the basic principle of the Torah. It is repeated in the New Testament, which calls it a fundamental law.

Of course, as we could expect, not everyone agreed with Rabbi Akiva. His usual disputant, Rabbi Ishmael argued that, on the contrary, the prohibition against idol worship is the fundamental Torah law. Maimonides (1138–1204) agreed with Rabbi Ishmael. Maimonides felt that idol worship was prohibited because it removes us from God. It causes us to focus on inconsequential matters that can not assist us in our, and society's, growth. Nevertheless, Rabbi Ishmael and Maimonides agreed that the *Leviticus* command is important.

What does it mean?
Despite its significance, the verse is problematical. How can one mandate or force "love"? It either comes of itself or it doesn't. We understand the word

"him" in 19:34; it refers to the stranger mentioned in that section. But who is a "neighbor" in *Leviticus* 19:18? Are non-Israelites included? Isn't it contrary to human nature to love another as much as one loves oneself? So what is God demanding? There are many different interpretations of the verse. We will describe four of them: the understandings of Maimonides, Nachmanides, ibn Ezra and Hillel.

Maimonides

In his *The Commandments*, Maimonides posits that the command applies only to Jews. The command obligates the Jew to want for others what he wants for himself; and whatever he does not want for himself, he should not want for others. The Maimonidean restriction, applying the rule only to Jews, would understandably upset people who would disagree with him.

Nachmanides

Nachmanides (1195–1270) recognized that it is impossible for most people to bestow as much love for another that one has for himself. Therefore, he concludes, this can not be the meaning of the verse. In fact, Rabbi Akiva teaches in the Babylonian Talmud *Baba Metzia* 62a that when one's life is in danger, concern for your own life takes precedence. Nachmanides, therefore, understands the command to instruct people not to be jealous. People should want others to have as much success as they hope for themselves. Curiously, Nachmanides failed to admit that in many instances it is impossible for people to wish another the same success he hopes for himself, especially if the two are striving for the same object.

Ibn Ezra

Abraham ibn Ezra (1089–1164) took another approach. He noted that the letter *lamed* that introduces *l'reiacha* is recognized as being superfluous and meaningless by many Bible commentators. However, he suggests that it may have its customary meaning of "to." Thus the passage may be stating, "You should love [that which is] *to* your neighbor [meaning, his possessions] as yourself [meaning, as if they were your own]." The command then is one that can be observed. It is to respect the possessions of another.

Hillel

Another interpretation that recognizes the limitations of human nature focuses on the fact that the Torah frequently chooses to dramatize its point by stating it in an exaggerated fashion, in hyperbole. Thus, for example, the Bible relates that the Tower of Babel reached all the way to heaven. It similarly describes the descendants of Abraham as being as numerous as the stars in the sky and the sand upon the beach. When Scripture describes some people as giants, it is probably telling us that they were mighty warriors.

The first century sage Hillel appears to have understood *Leviticus* 19:18 in this fashion. He gave a more practical and non-hyperbolic version of this command. In the Babylonian Talmud *Shabbat* 31a, he stated that the basic principle of Judaism is "What is hateful to you do not do to your neighbor."

Summary

The biblical law to love another as oneself was considered either the most basic principle of Judaism or one of the most basic. Yet it is difficult to understand, overly demanding and virtually impossible to implement. Maimonides suggested that it means that we should want others to have what we have, but added that the rule only applies to Jews, a notion that is difficult for many modern thinkers. Nachmanides contended that it proscribes jealousy. Ibn Ezra offered that it requires respect for another's possessions. Hillel recognized that the biblical wording was hyperbole and was not meant to be taken literally; it should be understood in its negative sense: do not do to others what we do not want others to do to us.

Emor

What is holiness?

The portion of *Emor* continues what some people call the Holiness Code, a part of the Bible that talks about holiness. It starts with *Leviticus* 19:2 which reports the divine command: "Be holy, for I the Lord your God am holy!" *Emor* includes laws such as priestly obligations and the laws of holidays.

Questions
1. What is holiness?
2. How did Eric Fromm define holiness?

What is holiness?
Various dissimilar answers to this question have been suggested. Some say that holiness means "separation": holy people are distinct and apart. Others propose that holiness is some undefined mystical state of piety, one of the top rungs of a ladder that religious people should climb and achieve. Still others offer a more down-to-earth idea of developing behavior that imitates how God, The Holy One, is portrayed as acting in the Bible, called *"imitatio deo."* For example, just as God is said to have visited Abraham when the patriarch was ill, so, too, people should visit the sick. Just as God is said to have buried Moses when no one else was around, so, too, people should perform this service.

How did Eric Fromm define holiness?
Eric Fromm, in his psychological work, *You Shall be as Gods,* presents another idea. He notes that variations of the Hebrew term *kadosh,* "holy," describe several Jewish ceremonies. A wedding service, for example, is called *kiddushin* even though the ritual is not magical. It does not and can not assure that the future relationship between the couple will be happy.

Why, then, is it called *kiddushin*? Fromm answers that *kiddushin* indicates that the relationship *can be* "holy" – that is, successful – if the couple works at making it so, if they do all that they can do. Fromm's theme, later adopted by the US Army, was: "Be all you can be!"

The same applies to the *kiddush*, the blessing over the wine that inaugurates the Sabbath meal. Neither the blessing nor the drinking of the wine has any magical effect upon the Sabbath or the family participating in it. The family needs to realize the potential of the Sabbath and act as tradition requires regarding the Sabbath. Then, they, not the ceremony, will turn the Sabbath into an experience of holiness.

Summary

Quite a few definitions have been offered for the term "holiness." These include a demand for separation, climbing mystical ladders, and copying what God homiletically and figuratively does. Eric Fromm suggested a psychological idea. Holiness is the recognition of the potential in man to create a situation that betters the individual, the family and society. When God ordered the Israelites to be holy, He was commanding them to work to achieve that potential. God created the world, but people must realize that they also have a duty to create, to be, in a sense, like God, see their capabilities and achieve them.

Behar

What is sin?

The biblical portion of *Behar*, like many other portions, warns the Israelites to observe God's commands. They are promised prosperity if they do so. They will, among other things, "dwell securely on the land" (*Leviticus* 25:18).

Questions
1. What is sin?
2. Is the emotional or the intellectual definition of sin healthier and more productive?

Definitions
Sin is a theological concept; it is seen as a transgression of divine law. It is the failure to act as one thinks God wants one to act. Most people's thinking and behavior regarding sin is wrong-headed, because it causes the person enormous emotional harm.

There are two ways to view sin. One is emotional and the other rational. The difference between the two is monumental and the impact that each makes upon its adherents is enormous and long lasting. The emotional approach generally carries a burden of unresolved guilt and at least some degree of internal discomfort. It diminishes the individual, rather than making him better. It destroys his future. The rational view, in contrast, helps him better himself. The first notion is unfortunately the one held by most people.

Freud
Although the psychologist Sigmund Freud prided himself on understanding religion in a rational manner, his approach to "sin" reflected the common emotional belief.

Freud discusses the feelings of guilt and sin, treating them as synonyms, in the final two chapters of his *Civilization and its Discontents,* first published in 1930. He contends that the feeling of sin/guilt is the reaction that a person sometimes feels for an act that he is thinking of doing or which he had already committed when he fears that the act will result in a loss of love.

For Freud, this need for love is basic, and the loss of love, or even the fear of loss, is detrimental, perhaps even catastrophic.

The problem starts, he insists, just after birth. The child recognizes that he is being protected by his father. Watching how his father reacts to him, he realizes that he needs to satisfy his father to get his love. He sees that when he does something contrary to his father's wishes, he loses this love. He decides to comply with his father's desires, and he begins to fear that he may make a mistake and act contrary to what his father wants from him. When he performs an alienating act and senses an estrangement from his father, he feels a loss of the love that he needs. This experience of alienation from love is, for Freud, the origin of what we call sin and guilt.

> At the beginning... what is bad is whatever causes one to be threatened with loss of love... one must avoid it. This, too, is the reason why it makes little difference whether one has already done the bad thing or one only intends to do it.

When the child begins to grow older, he does not lose the need for fatherly love. He may no longer be conscious of the need, but it is residing in his sub-conscious.

Since he is now older and has greater desires, Freud argues that he now requires a larger and more powerful father, and God fills this role in the life of the common man and woman. Knowing, as he did from childhood, that he must appease his father to attain his love and assistance, he makes all kind of appeasing gestures to God, the substitute for his father. When he fails to act as he believes God expects or plans such an act, he experiences a feeling of loss of love. Paradoxically, as Thomas D. Bernard wrote, "our sense of sin is in proportion to our nearness to God," the closer one is to God and the more one relies on His love, the greater the sense of sin and guilt. Freud wrote that sin:

...can best be identified as fear of loss of love. If he loses the love of another person upon whom he is dependent, he also ceases to be protected from a variety of dangers. Above all, he is exposed to the danger that this stronger person will show his superiority in the form of punishment.

According to Freud, the people of Israel considered themselves children of the Heavenly Father, God. When fate rained down misfortune upon them, the people's belief in their Father was not shaken. They saw the misfortune as divine displeasure at their misdeeds, at their failure to act as the Father demanded. Their fear of the loss of divine love was their feeling of sin. Some people tried to avoid this negative psychological experience by appeasing acts. But frequently the person was left with a fear that he may not have done enough. As a result, the fear continues despite the act of appeasement. This is not a healthy situation.

Other people attempted to avoid even the possibility of this feeling by isolating themselves from society and living the life of a hermit, believing that they were thereby forestalling any behavior that would estrange their Father. This is a largely ineffectual way of resolving the problem.

In short, the Freudian psychological view is a quasi-sophisticated way of understanding sin. It describes what the religious common man believes and the adverse impact that such a notion has upon the believer. Both Freud and the common man see sin as a "feeling," not an outward act; both understand that feeling as "guilt" with a permanent feeling of inadequacy coupled with enduring internal disabling unhappiness. Both portray man as childish, relying on a need for love of a father figure. Both see man reacting passively and fearfully. Neither recognizes a human obligation to do something to improve himself and society. Instead the guilt-ridden believer is shackled in an amorphous psychologically incapacitating bind that restricts him from useful and constructive behavior. "Sin," wrote Walter L. Carson, "is twisting and distorting out of its proper shape a human personality which God designed to be a thing of beauty and a joy forever." "The worst effect of sin is within," wrote Edwin Hubbell Chapin, "the disowned faculties...the low ideal, the brutalized and enslaved spirit."

A rational approach

A rational approach to sin avoids the obsessional destructive sense of guilt, its tormenting uneasiness and its unconscious call for punishment. Instead it shows people a positive attitude and a sense of direction toward a constructive future.

Surprising as it may sound, there is absolutely no concept of "sin" in the Hebrew Bible. The word *chet*, which is currently used for "sin," actually means "to miss the mark." When one commits a *chet*, he is attempting to reach a certain objective or goal and fails to attain it. It is like a person shooting an arrow at a target. After releasing the shaft, he looks and sees that the arrow missed the target.

What does a person do who has a goal and "missed the mark"? He does not sheepishly leave the tournament, psychologically devastated, with a feeling of guilt. He does not create a series of ceremonies to "atone" for his unsuccessful shot. Instead, he begins to consider why he had the disappointing result and what he can do to hit the target on his next shot. Then he takes bow and arrow in hand, aims in a better manner and shoots again.

The rational person examines his acts when it is reasonable to do so, and analyzes them to see if he attained his goals. When he finds that he "missed the mark," he questions why, devises a plan for the future and makes sure that when he does this act again, he does it right.

Repentance

Judaism has a concept of repentance. The rational concept of repentance fits well within a rational understanding of "sin." Maimonides, in his *Mishneh Torah, Hilchot Teshuvah* 2, states that repentance requires several steps. The individual must first recognize that he did something wrong. He must then realize that he would benefit by not doing it again. He then decides what the proper behavior should be. Finally, he finds a way to make it certain – probably, by developing new habits – that when the situation arises again he will act properly.

This concept of *chet* and repentance is totally mind oriented. The focus is on how he is going to act to benefit himself and society.

Summary

There are two basic concepts of "sin." The first is the commonly-held notion, which is also the view of many psychologists. Unfortunately, this idea produces a feeling of guilt and gives no sense of how to resolve the situation. The second recognizes that the individual simply made a mistake – he or she "missed the mark." This idea requires a person to recognize what he did wrong, decide not to do it again, decide what the proper behavior is and develop habits to assure that he or she will act properly in the future. The biblical portion of *Behar*, *Leviticus* 25, as well as many others, reminds us to observe God's commands. It tells us that we will benefit from the observance. Significantly, it does not threaten us with feelings of guilt in order to repent and perform as God desires. It also does not tell us that once we do wrong, we become shattered and psychologically ruined.

Bechukotai

Will God help us because of our ancestors?

Many people have a rather remarkable belief, what is called *zechut avot*, "merit of the ancestors." They read it in verses such as *Leviticus* 26:42, which suggests to them that God will remember the Israelite ancestors and treat their descendants well because of the ancestors' good behavior. "I will remember My covenant with Jacob, as well as My covenant with Isaac, and I will remember My covenant with Abraham."

Needless to say, this and similar passages, can be understood differently. God is simply saying that He will remember the promise He made to the ancestors, without the added notion that He is rendering good to the descendants because their forefathers and foremothers acted well. Be this as it may, the belief by many in *zechut avot* raises several questions.

Questions
1. What is *zechut avot*, "ancestral merit"?
2. Should one rely on his ancestor's merit rather than his own behavior?
3. Did all Jews in the past believe in ancestral merit?
4. How do some Jews show their belief in ancestral merit today?
5. If it worked in the past, does the merit of ancestors work today?

What is *zechut avot?*
The word *zechut*, "merit," neutral in origin, came to be charged with marked theological significance in later Jewish theology. The belief arose that a person's good deeds are credited to his "account," like putting money in the bank. The good deeds can be used/withdrawn by the individual or by others, by petition to God, in later periods when help is needed. In other words, when a person exhausted his own merits, he may benefit from *zechut avot*, "merits of the ancestors." The term "ancestors" is not restricted to the patriarchs, but refers

to the good behavior of any ancestor. This notion of the power of *zechut* is not in the Bible itself.

Moses Maimonides (1138–1204), in his *Guide of the Perplexed* 3:53, defines the biblical usage of *zechut* as "giving everyone his own due." For example, when Daniel states in 6:23, "My God sent His angel and shut the mouths of the lions, and they did not wound me because *merit* was found for me before Him," Daniel was not referring to the merit of his ancestors but his own.

When the extended concept was developed, many understood it literally. They relaxed, became passive and depended upon it to acquire aid that they did not deserve by vicarious reliance on the virtue of their predecessors. Others interpreted it symbolically. They saw it as a reminder and inspiration to act and imitate the proper behavior of their righteous ancestors.

When did the belief first manifest itself?

The extended understanding of *zechut* was mentioned for the first time by the sage Shemaiah in the first century B.C.E. He claimed that God divided the Red Sea for the Israelites in the days of Moses because of the *zechut* of Abraham. His fellow religious leader Avtalyon objected to this novel notion and insisted that it was the Israelites' own merit that saved them.

Examples

The Aramaic translation of the Pentateuch called *Targum Pseudo-Jonathan* (ninth or tenth century) has many midrashic supplements, and included the concept of *zechut avot* in about fifty verses. For example, *zechut* was used in the following situations according to this translator.

"Lot had sheep, cattle, and tents only through Abraham's *zechut*." (*Genesis* 13:5)

"The world was created solely on the *zechut* of Abraham's future good deeds." (*Genesis* 14:19)

"God will deliver Jews from their enemies on the account of Abraham's *zechut*." (*Genesis* 15:11)

"God listened to Ishmael's cry for help and saved him from dying of thirst because of Abraham's *zechut.*" (*Genesis* 21:17)

"Lavan's well flowed for twenty years due to Jacob's *zechut* and stopped flowing when Jacob left the country." (*Genesis* 31:22)

"Potiphar's household was blessed as payment for the *zechut* of Joseph who was the guardian over his household." (*Genesis* 39:5)

How do some people today show their belief in ancestral merit?

The most popular manifestation of this belief today is seen in the prayers that many Jews make at the graves of their parents. They pray that their parents will intercede for them with God. Many do so because they feel, albeit only unconsciously, that God will listen to their parents because of the merit of their good deeds, and that their parents' past good deeds will profit them today. Those who feel that one should rely only on their own behavior consider this practice wrong. They add that it reflects another mistaken notion, that we need someone else to intercede for us to God.

What is the current view of ancestral merit?

We noted above that the rationalist Maimonides rejected the idea of vicarious "ancestral merit" outright. He was not alone in maintaining this position. A number of other rabbis took another position. They felt that whereas *zechut* may have been effective in the past, it had ceased to work. Rabbi Joshua ben Levi, for example, argued that the merit of the patriarchs existed only until the time of the prophet Elijah. Abba bar Zavda stated that it stopped in the time of King Josiah. The Tosaphist Rabbeinu Tam, a grandchild of Rashi who lived in France in the twelfth century and was one of the great *halakhic* decision makers, stated that whatever ancestral merit existed has been exhausted.

Whether this was a diplomatic way that he and the others used to avoid the question whether it existed in the past is debatable, but what is apparent is that he and the other authorities were convinced that it does not exist today, and that reliance upon it is an abandonment of one's own responsibility and a descent into superstition. (See the Jerusalem Talmud, *Sanhedrin* 27d; the Babylonian Talmud, *Shabbat* 55a; and the Midrashim *Leviticus Rabbah* 36:5 and

Ecclesiastes Rabbah 12:8.) Needless to say, as with all Jewish concepts, since there is no Jewish catechism, we find people that maintain that the concept continues to work today.

Summary

Many people consciously or unconsciously subscribe to the notion that although they have no personal merit they can rely on divine help because of the merits of their ancestors. This is a belief that began in the first century B.C.E. Some individuals saw it hinted in the Bible in verses such as *Leviticus* 26:42. It was used by some Bible commentators to explain biblical occurrences and by other people to comfort those who felt that they lacked sufficient past good deeds of their own to merit heavenly assistance. The practice has been criticized for encouraging people to be passive about their own behavior. Three approaches still exist today. Some state that the notion of *zechut avot* never existed, some that it did exist in the past but hasn't worked for over 2,500 years, and some that it can still be relied on today.

Bamidbar

What did Nadav and Avihu do wrong?

The story of Nadav and Avihu, two of the four sons of Moses' brother the high priest Aaron, is repeated five times in Scriptures, in *Leviticus* 10:2, 16:1, *Numbers* 3:4, 26:61, and *I Chronicles* 24:2. In four of these five sites, both their offence and the punishment of death are reiterated. Yet despite the repetitions, it is unclear what they did, why they were punished, and what the punishment was.

Complicating the matter is that there is another narrative about 250 Israelite rebels that is similar to the episode of Aaron's two sons, both in the offense committed and in the punishment incurred.

The texts

The first appearance of the episode of Aaron's sons is *Leviticus* 10:1 and 2 and reads as follows: "Now Nadav and Avihu, the sons of Aaron, took each of them his censor, and put fire in it, and laid incense on it, and offered strange fire before the Lord, which He had not commanded them. And there came forth fire from before the Lord, and devoured them, and they died before the Lord."

The similar incident about 250 men who rebelled against Moses' leadership in the wilderness is told in *Numbers* 16:6, 7 and 35. God instructed Moses to put the rebels to a test. Each of them should "take censors... put fire in it, lay incense on it, before the Lord tomorrow; and it will be that the man whom the Lord chooses, he will be holy.... And fire came forth from the Lord, and devoured the 250 men that offered the incense."

Questions
1. What did Nadav and Avihu do wrong?
2. Did they act differently than the 250 rebels?
3. What is the significance of the punishment by fire in both cases?

What was the offense of Aaron's sons?

The Bible states that Nadav and Avihu brought "strange fire." Why was this wrong? The rabbis differed in identifying the fault.

For example, the Babylonian Talmud, *Eruvin* 63a, states that "the sons of Aaron died only because they gave a legal decision in the presence of their master Moses…. Although, they recognized that fire came down from heaven [as it states in 9:24, they decided that] it is a religious duty to bring also some ordinary fire."

The *Midrash Leviticus Rabbah* 20:6 has one sage present this idea, but in 20:8, another sage suggests four other reasons for their punishment. They entered the inner precincts of the sanctuary without permission, offered a sacrifice that they were not commanded to offer, brought fire from the kitchen, and failed to take counsel with one another before they acted.

In this same section, another sage states that the Bible repeats the story many times to inform us that "they were guilty of no other iniquity but this one alone," that they brought "strange fire."

Section 20:9 reports a sage saying that they died for four other reasons. They drank wine, did not wear all the prescribed priestly garments, did not wash their hands and feet before performing the service, and did not have children.

Section 20:10 has a tenth reason for their death, they were arrogant. This arrogance is explained in three ways, yielding a total of twelve descriptions of the event. They felt no woman was worthy to be their wife; they wanted Moses and Aaron to die so that they could assume authority over the community; and they looked at the *Shekhinah* (divine presence).

There are other sources, such as the *Midrash Sifra* that speculates that the sons brought a voluntary offering, one not ordered by God, to celebrate the dedication of the Tabernacle. Additionally, medieval commentators offer their own ideas. Nachmanides, for example, states that the two sons did not offer the sacrifice in a way that accomplished its purpose, a purpose understood by mystics. Rashbam suggests that the two sons were well meaning when they acted as they usually did and brought fire for the altar. However, Moses wanted the inauguration to be different, that no man-made fire should light the altar, but that it should be lit by a miraculous fire from God.

The punishment of Nadav and Avihu

The Babylonian Talmud, *Sanhedrin* 52a, relates that Nadav and Avihu died when four streams of fire issued from the Holy of Holies, entered their nostrils and killed them. The *Targum Pseudo-Jonathan*, which borrowed most of its material from the Talmuds and Midrashim, rendered the verse this way, "there came forth in anger from before the Lord a flame of fire that was divided into four threads. It entered [the four nostrils of] their noses and burned their souls; but their bodies were not burnt; and they died before the Lord."

Why fire?

Sanhedrin 52a emphasizes that the "souls" of Nadav and Avihu, as well as those of the 250 rebels, were burned, but not their bodies. "They incurred the punishment of fire to effect [the pollution of] their souls." It was their inner souls that caused them to act improperly, and so it was their souls that were burnt. This talmudic statement can be understood figuratively.

Summary

The tragic incident of Nadav and Avihu in *Leviticus* 10 and four other biblical sections does not specify the offense of Aaron's two sons.

Although more than a dozen diverse explanations of the offense of Aaron's sons are offered by the sages, a general theme runs through most of them. Aaron's sons were acting with misguided and over-enthusiastic religious intentions. Nadav and Avihu thought, for example, that it was proper to bring regular fire in addition to that which descended miraculously from God. They were eager to show what they considered suitable respect and love of God by offering an uncalled-for sacrifice. They rushed impetuously to worship God without due consideration and discussion with each other or with their father and uncle.

Their behavior was in this sense an act of misguided and over-enthusiastic zealotry similar to the poor judgment of the 250 Israelites who rebelled against Moses. While they saw their acts as well intended, they were still wrong.

Both groups behaved with fiery fervor for holy matters. They failed to realize that overzealousness and arrogance is far from appropriate in religion. It destroys the self and others.

The punishment for both fit their crime. A purifying fire burned their insides and left their bodies intact. The fire symbolized the inner nature of their offences, an over-fueled, midguided desire that had to be eradicated. It was fire fighting fire.

Nasso

Some comments on the priestly blessing

In *Numbers* 6:22–27, God instructs Moses to address his brother Aaron, the priest, and Aaron's children saying, "This is how you should bless the Israelites, say to them, 'May the Lord bless you and watch over you. May the Lord shine His face upon you and be gracious to you. May the Lord lift His face to you and give you peace.' Place My name on the Israelites and I will bless them."

This three-fold blessing raises many questions, including the following:

Questions
1. When is the blessing said?
2. Is God blessing the people or the priests, or are the people encouraged to bring blessings upon themselves?
3. How are the blessings implemented?
4. What is the meaning of each phrase in the blessing?

Some answers
Tradition states that the three-fold priestly blessing was recited twice daily in the ancient Tabernacle and Temples after the two biblically mandated daily sacrifices. When the second Temple was destroyed in the year 70 C.E., Rabban Yochanan ben Zakkai instituted the practice of having the priests recite it in the synagogue with certain solemnities. Among other things, he ordered the priests to stand in front of the synagogue congregation and recite the blessings bare-footed, just like the Temple priests, who wore no shoes while functioning in the Temple. This new practice highlighted for the people that the synagogue was now replacing the Temple. This was one of ten innovations that he introduced to transfer some of the Temple services into the synagogue. The innovations formed the nucleus of what would transform Pharisaic Judaism into Rabbinic Judaism. From that time on, the religious leaders who received proper training were called rabbis.

The priestly blessings are discussed in the *Mishnah Sotah* 7:1 where it states that it must be said in Hebrew. The Babylonian Talmud, *Sotah* 38–40 enumerates many other details. Among other things, the Talmud states that the blessings must be said after the priests washed their hands and when they raise their hands. They must speak loudly during the service to men, women and children. These and the other listed practices obviously generated a recital with solemnity and impressed the people with its significance.

Today, although most synagogues have the priests recite the blessing, they differ when it is done. In Israel it is generally said daily, while in the diaspora, it is recited only on holidays.

The blessings were never meant to imply that the priests are blessing the people. The sentence following the blessing explicitly states that God "will bless them." It was also never intended to suggest that God blesses the people only because the priests are reminding Him to do so or prompting Him. The priests' function is to remind the people who are listening to work on their own to bring about the blessings.

Many suggestions are offered to explain the meaning of the blessings. The ancient, probably fourth century, *Midrash Sifra,* states that the first refers to material prosperity, such as food, clothing and health. The words "watch over you" mean guard you from theft of these items. The second addresses the understanding of the Torah, for true illumination is derived from the Torah. The third asks for God's mercy, for treatment beyond what one's behavior merits.

Virtually all the commentators recognize that the anthropomorphic word God's "face" should not be taken literally, because God does not have a face like a human. It denotes the way humans perceive God interacting with them.

Commenting on the second blessing, regarding Torah, Sforno (born about 1470) reminds us of the rational idea that one needs to use his intelligence: May God open the eyes of the congregants to be able to see the wonders of the Torah and understand the marvels of this world.

Showing respect to people

The Babylonian Talmud, *Sotah* 40a, relates that the manner in which the blessings are made confirms that it is more important to show deference for people than for God.

The priests are told to face the congregation in the Synagogue and turn their backs on the Ark that holds the Torah scrolls. This draws the congregation's attention to the fact that regard for the needs of the congregants is more essential than consideration for and esteem of the Torah and God.

Rabban Yochanan ben Zakkai's institution that the priests bless bare-footed (or at least without shoes) was seen by some rabbis as another demonstration of this lesson of respect for people. The priest was protected from insult. If he wore shoes, they may become untied, and the people might embarrass him with derisive taunts for his undignified appearance.

Summary

The priestly blessings are more than a petition. The priests were instructed to stand before the congregants with detailed prescribed solemnity to impress upon them that they must work to bring blessing in their own and their family's lives. This was a Temple ceremony that was intentionally incorporated into the synagogue worship service to emphasize the idea that despite the Temple's destruction and other adversities, one has a duty to carry on. The central blessing, after the one for basic human needs and before the expression of the desire for peace, is the request for illumination, an understanding of Torah and an intellectual grasp of the functioning of the universe and how humans can use it properly, to profit themselves and society.

But climbing the ladder of learning *per se* is insufficient. The manner in which the blessings were recited reminds us that appreciation for and consideration of other people is more important than reverence of learning and appreciation of God. Or, stated differently, respect for God is demonstrated by how His creatures are treated.

Maimonides vs. Aristotle on the Golden Mean and humility

Numbers 12:3 informs us that "the man Moses was very humble, more than any person on the face of the earth." The *Midrash Sifre* elaborates: although Moses' humility did not hinder him from confronting Pharaoh and demanding the release of the Israelites from the horrors of Egyptian slavery, when it came to his own life, he listened humbly and refused to defend himself from the criticism of his sister and brother who censored him regarding his wife.

Questions
1. What is the "golden mean"?
2. How does humility fit into the "golden mean"?

Maimonides and Aristotle
There are areas of thought where Maimonides (1138–1204) agreed with much of what the Greek philosopher Aristotle (384–322 B.C.E.) taught. This included Aristotle's basic ethical teaching of the "golden mean," that people should develop habits of behavior according to the middle course between two extremes. However, he did disagree on a few items, one of which was that he felt that the golden mean did not apply to humility.

Aristotle
Aristotle deemed the modest man a ridiculous violator of the golden mean. He was untruthful if he was wise but claimed otherwise. He was a fool if he let modesty keep him from his due. In his *Necomachean Ethics* 4:3, Aristotle wrote:

> The unduly humble man, being worthy of good things, robs himself of what he deserves, and seems to have something bad about him from the fact that he does not think himself worthy of good things, and

seems to not know himself; else he would have desired the things he was worthy of, since these are good.

The Aristotelian view reflected the ancient Greek oracle. For atop the temple of Delphi, one of the instructive maxims besides "Know thyself" was "Nothing overmuch."

Maimonides

Maimonides, in contrast, stated that the modest person is acting properly. He discussed the value of the golden mean in many places, especially in his *Shemoneh Perakim* chapter 4, his *Mishneh Torah Hilchot Deot* chapter 2, and his commentary to *Pirke Avot* 4:4. In essence, he states:

1. Proper conduct is the middle path "between two extremes, each of which is unfavorable: one is excess and the other restriction." "For example," he explains, "restraint is the middle path between indulgence and the absence of desire…. Similarly, generosity is the median between stinginess and extravagance." A person acquires the proper character trait by habituating himself to action according to the golden mean.

2. When a person sees that he is improperly leaning to one extreme, he should immediately correct his actions by conducting himself according to the other extreme until he feels certain that "an equilibrium is established. Once he reaches equilibrium, he should turn away from the other extreme" and follow the proper middle path. For example, if a person developed miserly characteristics, he should "spend freely constantly…until he has driven out the miserly character trait." It is necessary to take this extreme measure because a shift to the middle path of generosity would not be sufficient to "cure his affliction."

3. There are several exceptions to the second rule. These include pride, anger, improper speech, jesting and greed. These are such exceptionally bad qualities that "it is proper to distance himself from these qualities as much as possible by adopting behavior at the opposite extreme." In regard to pride, Maimonides suggests, it is proper to "act lowly and unassuming. This is why it is said about Moses that he was 'very humble,' not just 'humble.'"

Maimonides recognized that virtually everyone is prideful and that it is extremely difficult to eradicate this emotion. Since pride is so inappropriate and reprehensible, Maimonides agreed with the rabbis in the Babylonian Talmud, *Sotah* 4b, that whoever is arrogant acts as if he denies God. The rabbis recognized that God created everyone in "His image" and that one shows that he denies this fact when he treats others unsuitably.

*   *   *

My late father Rabbi Dr. Nathan Drazin was a brilliant man, and although recognized as such, he was very humble. For example, father knew the entire Torah by heart, but never showed off his knowledge.

Father asked how it is possible to be both truthful and humble. The Torah tells us to be both. But if a person knows that he is smart, how can he be humble when he is supposed to be truthful?

Father answered that a truly smart man understands that other people know things that he does not know. Thus it is truthful and proper for a person to act humbly toward all people.

*   *   *

The only wisdom we can hope to acquire is the wisdom of humility.
       –T. S. Eliot

Deriving lessons from apparently superfluous biblical words

Numbers 13:2 begins with the words *shelach lecha,* "send." God tells Moses to send men, one from each of the twelve tribes, to spy out Canaan and ascertain if the land can be conquered. The Torah could have used just the single word *shelach,* instead of the combined form, to say "send." The dual form *shelach lecha* appears only here in Scripture. The word *lecha* is added to *lech,* "go," in *Genesis* 12:1 and 22:2, and in both incidences adds no additional meaning to *lech:* the dual form *lech lecha* means simply "go."

Questions
1. How do the Talmud and Rashi interpret the Bible's seemingly superfluous word?
2. What are the views of Rabbi Akiva and Rabbi Ishmael on this subject?
3. How does Abraham ibn Ezra deal with this subject?
4. What is an *asmachta?*

The Talmud and Rashi
The Babylonian Talmud, *Sotah* 34b, reads the term *shelach lecha* literally, not as a two word idiom expressing the single idea "send," but "send to you [or, for yourselves]," since *lecha* by itself means "to you." The Talmud observes that God had already assured the Israelites that they could conquer Canaan successfully. Therefore there was no need for scouts to ascertain and confirm that Canaan was conquerable. However, when the people arrogantly ignored God's assurance and said (as reported in *Deuteronomy* 1:22) we want to send spies, God acquiesced to the request and said *shelach,* "send." But, He added, do so *lecha,* "for yourselves," emphasizing that this was not a favorable initiative.

Rashi (1040–1105) expands upon the Talmud's idea. He adds that just as Moses' sister Miriam underwent dire consequences because she spoke derogatorily about Moses, so, too, the people suffered when they spoke improperly. Miriam was stricken with leprosy, a disease that the rabbis associated with malicious speech. The Israelites were also punished because they showed by their speech that they were still a slave-minded people unsuited for settlement in Canaan. God kept these insufficiently developed Israelites in the desert for forty years until a new generation of Israelites arose with a mind-set to conquer the land.

The views of Rabbi Akiva and Rabbi Ishmael

The Talmud and Rashi are using the interpretation methodology of Rabbi Akiva when they rely on the single word *lecha* for this interpretation. Rabbi Akiva was convinced that since the Torah emanated from God and since God is perfect, He would not add unnecessary words when He spoke. Thus the additional *lecha* must be suggesting an additional thought.

This methodology is contrary to that of Rabbi Ishmael. Rabbi Ishmael felt that despite its origin, the Torah needs to communicate and can only do so if people understand what is being said. Thus, the Torah must speak in human language. Since humans frequently add words for various reasons, such as for the sake of emphasis or simply to create a beautiful phrase, the Torah does so as well. Rabbi Ishmael would see the phrase *shelach lecha* as an idiom, two words saying one thing "send," nothing more.

Abraham ibn Ezra

Rabbi Ishmael's point is repeated by many commentators, such as the rationalist ibn Ezra (1189–1164) in his commentary to *Exodus* 20. In this commentary, he rejects the talmudic explanation of the differences in language between the Decalogue of Exodus 20 and *Deuteronomy* 5. Among other things, some rabbis maintained that *Exodus* uses *zachor* ("remember") and *Deuteronomy*, *shamor* ("keep"), because "God said both words simultaneously." Ibn Ezra pointed out that this is unreasonable. If God would have done so, the people who were listening would be hearing an incomprehensible sound. Like Rabbi Ishmael, he insisted that the Torah needs to speak so that people can understand. (He explained that the *Exodus* version is the original divine revelation and the one in *Deuteronomy* is the interpretation of Moses.)

Genesis 12:1

Rabbi Ishmael's view can be seen to be reasonable when we examine the two other incidences were *lecha* is added to *lech*, "send." In *Genesis* 12:1, God instructs the patriarch Abraham to leave his homeland and travel to Canaan. He says *lech lecha*, "go." Now if the word *lecha* is added, as *Sotah* 34b and Rashi insist, to indicate that the trip is being made on Abraham's initiative, but God was dissatisfied with the journey, this would not make any sense whatsoever. It is quite evident from the total context, and no one disagrees, that God wanted Abraham to go to Canaan and wanted his descendants to settle there.

Genesis 22:2

Genesis 22:2 is similar. God instructs Abraham to take his beloved son Isaac and travel to Mount Moriah to sacrifice his son on the mountain. He commands him *velech lecha*, "and go." Here, too, it would be unreasonable to say that that God did not want Abraham to take the trip, He was clearly commanding him to do so.

An *asmachta*

Didn't the talmudic sages and Rashi understand that *shelach lecha* and *lech lecha* could be idioms for "send" and "go," with no added significance to the attached *lecha*? Didn't they know that they could not use this interpretation in the two *Genesis* verses? Of course they knew this. They were very wise and they knew the Torah. Then why did they give their interpretation?

There is a principle of interpretation known as *asmachta*, "support": using a scriptural text to support a rabbinical idea, even though a plain reading of the text does not conform to the teaching. When the rabbis use an *asmachta*, they understood that the lesson is not contained in the biblical source, but the biblical verse or word is used by the rabbis to add a sense of importance to the idea or as a tool to help the student remember the lesson.

Thus, the rabbis are not telling us what the text states. They are informing us how they understood the motivation lying behind the trip of the spies in *Numbers* 13:2. They are informing us that this motivation was wrongheaded because God had assured the Israelites that they could conquer the land and it was more than presumptuous for them to insist on observing the land.

Additionally, by using the *asmachta,* they emphasized that the lesson of *Numbers* 13:2 must be taken to heart and remembered whenever we, the Bible readers, act. The lesson is that there are consequences to our behavior. The consequences to the exploration of Canaan affected an entire generation of Israelites who, as a result of their mistake, died in the desert.

Rashi expresses this idea when he explains why the story of the spies follows the story of Miriam's slander of her brother Moses. The joining of the episodes, Rashi states, warns us not to repeat the error of the spies. They saw Miriam punished for evil talk and failed to learn from what occurred to her.

Summary

There are two basic approaches to interpreting Scripture. The followers of Rabbi Akiva insist that every biblical word is significant because each was dictated by God who certainly would not use superfluous language. In contrast, the students of Rabbi Ishmael focused on the fact that the Bible was given to humans in a language that they could understand. Therefore, unnecessary language can be found frequently in the Bible for emphasis, because of idioms, or to beautify the language.

The two rabbis interpret seemingly supplementary words differently. The first seeks a lesson in the extra words. The second does not.

Additionally, we saw another method used by the ancient rabbis in commenting on the Torah and teaching lessons, *asmachta.* Even though the rabbis realized that the words or phrases may not imply a certain lesson, they attach a teaching to it as a learning tool to emphasize the teaching and as an aid to remember it.

Korach

Does the Bible record incidences chronologically?

The traditional rabbinically accepted Bible commentators disagree on a fundamental issue: whether the Bible records events chronologically. Each view affects how the incident should be understood. Each sees different motivations for the occurrence and dissimilar outcomes. The divergent views may also result in radically unlike philosophies of Judaism. There are many examples of this phenomenon. We will examine two of them.

Questions

1. What are the various views concerning biblical chronology?
2. Do the commentators disagree in interpreting the stories of Korach and the Tabernacle?

When did the episode of Korach occur?

Numbers 16 recounts the episode of Korach's and a couple of hundred cohorts' rebellion against Moses and Aaron while the Israelites were in the wilderness. The underlying complaint of the rebels is unclear. We have only a short account of their grievance – a single sentence in Hebrew – and scholars debate its meaning. The 1962 translation of the Jewish Publication Society of America renders it: "You [Moses and Aaron] have gone too far! For all the community are holy, all of them, and the Lord is in their midst. Why then do you raise yourselves above the Lord's congregation?"

When did this confrontation occur? What prompted it? What did the rebels want? We will examine two approaches. Both are based on how they address the question "Does the Bible record events chronologically?"

Abraham ibn Ezra

The rationalistic Spanish Bible commentator Abraham ibn Ezra (1089–1164) was convinced – like the Babylonian Talmud, *Pessachim* 6b – that the Bible occasionally records occurrences out of chronological sequence. He thought that it was reasonable to assume that Korach's chicanery occurred in the wilderness of Sinai. Korach was provoked when Moses displaced the Israelite first-born sons from performing priestly duties with the Levites, and when he elevated Aaron and his sons to the position of priests. This occurred in *Numbers* 8:5–22. The first-borns lost the priestly role when they showed their unworthiness by participating in the affair of the golden calf. Prior to this debacle, the first-borns were tribal leaders who performed priestly functions, as indicated in *Exodus* 13:2 and 19:22.

Ibn Ezra imagines that there were many Israelites who suspected that Moses made the decision out of spite, or nepotism, without a divine mandate, solely on his own initiative. Korach and his fellow Levite conspirators were incensed that they were degraded to the role of assistants to Moses' elder brother Aaron. Korach was especially enraged because he was both a first-born and a Levite (as indicated in *Exodus* 6:21). He argued vociferously that Aaron was no more appropriate for the role of high priest than any other Levite, such as he, because "all the community are holy."

Datan and Aviram and their group, fellow conspirators from the tribe of Reuben, according to ibn Ezra, joined Korach because they were incensed because Moses elevated Joshua of the tribe of Ephraim to be his assistant and divided the tribe of Joseph into two, thereby giving them a double portion in the land of Canaan. They felt that these honors should have gone to their own first-born tribe, Reuben.

Nachmanides

Nachmanides (1195–1270) disagreed. He insisted that the Torah is written in a chronological sequence except when it explicitly states otherwise, and even then the sequence is only changed when there is a compelling reason for doing so. He therefore places the Korach flare-up in the wilderness of Paran, after the spies were sent by Moses to scout out Canaan and determine if it was conquerable.

Nachmanides contends that Korach was infuriated because Moses promoted Elizaphan to be head of the Kahathites, and not him. He was also jealous of Aaron. Datan and Aviram, according to Nachmanides, joined the revolt because of their complaint that Moses took the people out of Egypt into the water-less desert, where they will certainly die, since the spies had just reported that the Israelites could not defeat the Canaanites.

Nachmanides recognized that all of the incidences that he mentioned occurred much earlier. But he argued that, although unstated in Scripture, the conspirators were provoked now and not earlier because of several other dire things. They saw people burned at Taverah (11:13), that many died at Kivrot-hataavah (11:34), and they noticed that Moses did not entreat God to renounce his decision to punish the entire nation because of their reaction to the negative report of the spies (14:26–39). They could not understand why Moses did not beseech God to annul the devastating decree. Sensing the embitterment of the people, Nachmanides argues, Korach and his core group of rebels saw that this was an opportune time to express their grievances and gain some national support.

By placing the Korach rebellion after the experience of the golden calf and by explaining the complaints of the mutineers as an opposition to their punishment, their loss of leadership and the priestly privileges, ibn Ezra is able to describe their behavior without difficulty. Nachmanides' approach, on the other hand, requires one to imagine matters that are not stated in Scripture; as he himself admits when he call his explanation *derash,* not the obvious and clear meaning of the text.

When was the Tabernacle built?
Nachmanides vs. Rashi

Nachmanides also insisted in his commentaries to different verses that other commentators are wrong in saying that the Torah sometimes presents incidences outside of chronological order. A significant example, one that effects the way one answers the question "Did God want the Tabernacle?" is found in Nachmanides' commentary to *Leviticus* 8:2.

Nachmanides strongly dissents from Rashi's (1040–1105) view in *Exodus* 31:18 on the issue of chronological sequence. Rashi wrote that the incident of the golden calf in *Exodus* 32 preceded the commandment to build the Tabernacle, which begins in *Exodus* 25. Nachmanides is adamant that since chapter 25 precedes 32, Rashi has the events backward.

What difference does this make? The disagreement addresses whether God wanted the Tabernacle or He only allowed it because the immature Israelites needed it.

If the Tabernacle was constructed, as Rashi contends, after the Israelites demonstrated though building the calf that they needed a physical presence and sacrifices to show their love of God, we would see that the Tabernacle was constructed to address these human needs and not because God wanted it. If, on the other hand, God instructed the building of the Tabernacle before the people worshipped with the calf, as Nachmanides insisted in his commentary to *Leviticus* 1:9, it would appear that it had been built because God wanted it and, as Nachmanides also states, needed it.

Maimonides

Maimonides (1138–1204) takes the position contrary to that of Nachmanides in his *Guide of the Perplexed* 3:32. He explains that God does not require or want sacrifices, but God allowed it because the as-yet undeveloped people needed it. In the translation of M. Friedlander, he wrote:

> the custom which was in those days general among men, and the general mode of worship in which the Israelites were brought up, consisted in sacrificing animals in those temples which contained certain images, to bow down to the images, and to burn incense to them.… It was in accordance with the wisdom and plan of God, as displayed in the whole creation, that He did not command us to give up and discontinue these manners of service, for to obey such a commandment it would have been contrary to the nature of man, who generally cleaves to that which he is used.

Maimonides warns us not to suppose that God could have resolved the problem by changing man's nature, "the nature of man is never changed by miracles." He states clearly, "the prophets thus distinctly declared that the object of the sacrifices is not very essential, and God does not require them."

Summary

There is disagreement among the biblical commentators as to whether or not the Bible records events in chronological order. This disagreement can effect the way we understand biblical episodes, the motivation of its characters and how we should interpret events to inspire our own lives. This disagreement can also color how we view fundamental issues of Judaism, such as whether God desires sacrifices.

Chukat

The curious story of the judge Yiftach

The haptarah for the portion of *Chukat* is *Judges* 11, an episode in the extraordinary life of the judge Yiftach. The "judges" in the book of *Judges* may not have had a judicial function. None of them are portrayed explicitly performing the judicial role, although the judicial function may be implied for figures such as Samuel in *I Samuel* 7:7 and for Deborah in *Judges* 4 and 5, according to Rashi and Radak.

The judges functioned as *ad hoc* leaders, arising because of the exigencies of the time to lead the people, or parts of them, in military battles against enemies that were oppressing the dis-united Israelite tribes. Scholars generally understand the book's term "judge" to denote a "charismatic leader." If it does refer to a judicial function, the book may be stating that God, not a human, was judging the people through these "judges." Most of the judges performed remarkable, even uncommon feats, but two stand out as especially unusual, one was Samson and the other Yiftach.

The story of Yiftach in Judges 11

Yiftach was born in Gilead to a prostitute and was raised by his father, but his father's wife's children tossed him out of the parental home. Yiftach journeyed to another country where he was joined by a band of men who "went out with him." The latter phrase is obscure, like much else in the story, but presumably means that they engaged in illegal raids.

When the warring nation Ammon attacked the Israelite city Gilead, the elders rushed to the outcast and pleaded that he lead their defense, probably because of the skills that he had developed during his raids. Yiftach chided them for joining his brothers when they expelled him from his home. After further talk, he agreed to lead the battle if they would make him their ruler. The elders agreed, swore that they would do so, and the oath was announced publicly.

Yiftach tried diplomatic negotiations with the Ammonite king, which included a review of the history of the relations between the Ammonite and Israelite people, without success. Then, before going out to war, he swore an oath: "If the people of Ammon are given over to me, then whatever goes out from the door of my house to me when I return in peace from the Ammonites shall be for the Lord. I will sacrifice it as a burnt offering."

Yiftach fought Ammon and was victorious. When he returned home, his daughter, an only child, greeted him with a victory ceremony, playing a musical instrument and dancing. Yiftach looked on in shock and tore his cloths in mourning. He told his daughter of his vow and insisted that he must keep it. His daughter agreed that he must do so. However, she requested that she be allowed to delay its execution for two months while she and her friends descended the mountain and bewailed the loss of her virginity. Then "he did with her according to his vow that he made."

Questions

The story of Yiftach raises quite a few questions, including the following:

1. Why did Yiftach make his unusual oath?
2. Why didn't he nullify the oath when he saw what had happened?
3. What happened to his daughter?
4. Does the Torah portion connected to the Haphtarah help answer the questions?

Can the questions be answered?

What makes the story of Yiftach so fascinating is that the text itself offers no answers to any of these questions. Both ancient and modern scholars suggest solutions, but their resolutions are no better than speculations. A reader should examine the story and seek his own understanding. He can view each detail from a religious, moral, psychological, social, literary or other angle, if he chooses. He may want to consider the following thoughts:

1. The name Yiftach is derived from *phathah*, which means "open." With the opening letters, it denotes "God opens." Ironically, chapter 11 relates incidences that are far from open.

2. The tale concerns unnamed brothers who banish Yiftach, and he, in turn, banishes or kills (we will discuss this below) his unnamed daughter.

3. With chapter 12, the narration depicts three family conflicts. Yiftach is pushed out by his brothers, he cuts off his daughter and, in chapter 12, he kills tens of thousands of fellow Israelites of the tribe of Manasheh.

4. Yiftach was selected to lead the people after the elders swore that they would make him their ruler. When the conflict with Ammon started, this oath by the elders, which affected his future status, was on his mind, and he made one of his own. He may not have wanted to break his vow fearing that if he did so the elders would see that they can nullify their oath.

5. Offering a sacrifice in relation to a battle was a commonplace practice for some people and Yiftach was complying with this ritual. He thereby showed his reliance on God. He expected that an animal would be the first to rush out to him when he returned, since the animals were in the field surrounding his home. Ironically, his daughter, following another long tradition, went out with ceremony to greet him, and met her disastrous end.

6. Don Isaac Abravanel, Rabbeinu Geshon, Radak and Metzudat David cite the Babylonian Talmud, *Taanit* 4a, and the *Midrashim Genesis Rabbah* and *Leviticus Rabbah* and suggest that Yiftach could have had his vow annulled by the High Priest Pinchas. However, he felt that because of his new leadership position he should not take the initiative and go to the High Priest, but Pinchas should come to him. Pinchas, in turn, acted equally foolishly, demanding that because of his spiritual position Yiftach should approach him. Their arrogance resulted in the death of Yiftach's daughter.

The sages do not discuss the irony that both Pinchas (in the Torah) and Yiftach performed zealous acts for what they considered to be pious reasons, and some commentators criticize both of them for their behavior, Yiftach for his vow and Pinchas for killing the man who had public sex during an idolatrous orgy without a judicial hearing (*Numbers* 25).

7. Some commentators argue that Yiftach sacrificed his daughter as he had vowed. They say that the Bible does not state this explicitly – but uses the words "He did to her as he had vowed" – because it was considered too repulsive an act for the Bible to state openly.

8. Some of the commentators state that although sacrificing children is strictly prohibited, as stated in *Jeremiah* 7:31, Yiftach and some other judges

were so entangled with pagan notions that he did not realize that his act was wrong.

9. Some commentators, relying on the Talmud and Midrashim, have an interesting contrary interpretation of the entire event. They contend that Yiftach never vowed to offer whatever exited his house as a sacrifice. By translating the *vav* in his final sentence as "or," instead of "and," which is its meaning in many verses, they understand Yiftach saying: "I will sacrifice whatever exits my house if it is fit for a sacrifice. However (or), if it is unfit, such as a human or a dog, I will dedicate that item to God." Thus, since his daughter came to meet him, she had to be dedicated totally to God; that is, she had to live alone in a cloistered manner.

In fact, Abravanel suggests this episode as the origin and paradigm for the Christian idea to cloister females. Thus, he continues, Yiftach's daughter requested a stay of two months while she could wander around and see the world for the last time before she was secluded from society. She also asked for this time to "bewail her virginity." By this, she meant that she was bewailing the fact that she would never be able to see or marry a man in the future.

Does the biblical portion of *Chukat* provide an answer?
Two reasons stand out as to why the sages selected the Yiftach account as the Haphtarah of the biblical portion of *Chukat*.

1. Yiftach's negotiation with the Ammonite king focused on how the Israelites captured the land that had once belonged to the Ammonites from the Moabites, who had taken it from them. He referred to incidences that are recorded in the portion of *Chukat*. Thus the accounts are related.

2. The chapters of *Chukat* contain laws that some sages consider inscrutable or difficult to understand. Those who chose the Yiftach account may have wanted to suggest that the story of Yiftach is as obscure as many laws in *Chukat,* and we can only guess the answers to the questions that the tale raises.

Summary
The chronicle of Yiftach's remarkable life raises many imponderables, including why he made such an outrageous oath, why he failed to have the oath nullified,

and how he fulfilled his outrageous vow on his daughter. The biblical text offers no answers. It does not even hint at a solution. One can only speculate.

It is possible that the sages selected the tale of Yiftach as the Haphtarah of the portion of *Chukat* because they recognized that *Chukat* has important laws that are difficult to understand, and they wanted to highlight that the story of Yiftach is also obscure, but that it is worth-while trying to unravel it.

Balak

What is the Jewish view toward the non-Israelite prophet Baalam?

Many Synagogue attendees, if not most, listen attentively to their rabbi's sermon and imagine that there is only one interpretation of a biblical verse or incident, the one mentioned by the rabbi. They would be amazed to learn that there are verses and incidences where the ancient sages not only disagree about the interpretation, but even have totally contrary views.

An example is the story of the non-Israelite prophet Balaam. There is no consensus in the ancient Jewish sources as to whether he was a good or bad man, and whether he was a sorcerer or a prophet.

Questions
1. What does the Bible tell us about Balaam?
2. Do some Scripture commentators consider Balaam a good man while others take the contrary view?
3. Was Balaam a prophet?

The scant biblical description of Balaam
The story of Balaam is narrated in a few biblical sources. It is mentioned in *Numbers* in chapters 22–24 and 31:15–16. A brief neutral recollection is also in *Deuteronomy* 23:5–6, *Joshua* 24:9–10, *Nehemiah* 13:1–2 and *Micah* 6:5. The recollections only recall that Balaam attempted to curse the Israelites, but that God turned the curses into blessings. No value judgment is made.

Negative depictions of Balaam
The view of the first Jewish philosopher Philo
The first written value judgment of Balaam's character is contained in Philo (about 20 B.C.E.–50 C.E.). In *Vita Mosis*, he is pictured as a liar and a

hypocrite. Despite Balaam's claims, God never appeared to him at all. In *VM* 52.287:

> the seer proved himself to be even worse than the king…he pressed forward even more readily than his conductor [the king who hired him], partly because he was dominated by the worst of vices and conceit, partly because in his heart he longed to curse, even if he were prevented from doing so with his voice.

The New Testament

There are three New Testament passages that discuss Balaam: 2 *Peter* 2:15–16, *Jude* 11, and *Revelations* 2:14. They disparage the seer as willing to sin because of greed for salary (*Peter* and *Jude*) and that he led the Israelites to eat food sacrificed to idols, and to fornication (*Revelations*).

The treatment of Balaam by early Bible translators

The Palestinian *Targums*, the translations of the Bible into Aramaic that were composed in Israel, expand upon the pejorative descriptions. The *Targum* called *Neophyti* describes Balaam as "wicked." It states that he lacked understanding, and charged him with taking advantage of his employer's messengers (in 22:30). Balaam admits in the expanded *Targumic* version of the story that because of his behavior he expects to have no portion in the world to come in (23:10). He is depicted as being so depraved that he set up his daughters as prostitutes (24:25). Yet in 24:3 and 15, *Neophyti* ironically praises Balaam as being more honorable than his father and surprisingly states that "what has been hidden from all the other prophets has been revealed to him."

The Aramaic Translation *Pseudo-Jonathan* identifies Balaam as Lavan the Aramean, the uncle of Jacob and father of Jacob's wives Leah and Rachel. He was insane because of the burden of his abundant knowledge (22:5). He had no pity for the Israelites despite their being his descendants (22:5). His own ass ridiculed him and called him a fool, criticized him for deceiving Balak's messengers, and reminded him that he, the ass, had given Balaam carnal pleasure (22:30). Nevertheless, this *Targum* praises Balaam, as does *Neophyti*, in 24:3–4 and 15, for being more glorious than his father and for knowing dark mysteries that were hidden from other prophets. Balaam in this *Targum*'s enlarged version of the episode advised Balak to use seductive women to ensnare the Israelites. He should place them in inns where food and drink are sold inexpensively, so that the Israelites would be enticed to come, have sexual intercourse with them and reject God (24:14, 25, 31:8). He was later killed by Moses' bother's grandson Pinchas when he tried to escape by flying through the air with magical incantations. Pinchas, according to this *Targum,* was able to fly and pursue Balaam because he pronounced God's holy name. Pinchas flew after Balaam, seized him by the head, pulled him down to earth, and slew him with his sword.

The Mishnah's view

The *Mishnah Avot* 5:19 continues the disparaging and insulting portrait of the prophet. It contrasts "the wicked" Balaam, who has an evil eye, a proud soul, and a haughty mind, with the patriarch Abraham, who has a good eye and a humble soul.

The Talmud expands upon the Mishnah

The Babylonian Talmud, *Sanhedrin* 105a–106b, is similarly insulting. It states that the name Balaam denotes his character. He is either *belo am,* "without a people" – meaning he has no portion in the world-to-come with other people, or *blm,* "he devoured [or corrupted] a people." He is identified, as in *Pseudo-Jonathan,* with Lavan the Syrian. His father was a prophet, but Balaam's powers were greater. He was reduced from being a prophet to a soothsayer as a punishment for trying to curse Israel. He was wicked. He was blind in one eye and limped on one foot. He practiced enchantment by means of his membrum. He committed bestiality with his ass. Although he offered forty-two sacrifices for an unworthy purpose, to enable him to curse Israel, he was nevertheless rewarded with the privilege of having Ruth, the ancestor of King David, as his descendant. Balaam advised King Balak how to entice the young Israelite males. He later returned to Balak demanding payment for the twenty-four thousand Israelites who were destroyed by a divine plague through his advice. He was present when the Israelites slew the Midianite kings and was killed with them. He was thirty years old when he was killed. The story is in other books of the Babylonian Talmud: *Baba Bathra* 15b, *Avodah Zarah* 4a–b, *Taanit* 20a, and in the Jerusalem Talmud *Sotah* 5:8, 20b.

A Midrash is similar

The *Midrash Numbers Rabbah* 20:6 also slights Balaam. It states that God "raised up Moses for Israel and Balaam for the idolaters," but it called Balaam a despicable person, "a vessel full of urine." He destroyed his soul by going to help King Balak (20:11).

Portrayals of Balaam in a favorable manner
Pseudo-Philo

Balaam appears in a good light, as a tragic hero in the early biblical interpreter, the *Liber Antiquitatum Biblicarum* of *Pseudo-Philo*. Balaam has no antipathy for the Israelites, no greed, and no sympathy for Moab's cause. His only wish is to do God's will. He was deceived by King Balak whom he pitied. Finally, realizing his mistake, and that he had no chance to return to God's favor, he committed spiritual suicide by giving evil advice to Balak.

Midrash Sifre

The *Midrash Sifre*, like *Pseudo-Philo*, is also complimentary. It states that although no Israelite prophet compared to Moses, the non-Israelite Balaam was comparable and was greater in three respects. Moses, according to this Midrash, did not know who spoke with him or when the vision would occur, but Balaam knew these facts. Moses, according to this Midrash, had to stand when he received prophecy, while Balaam was able to relax by lying down.

Targum Onkelos

In contrast to the Palestinian Targums, the authoritative, rabbinically accepted early fifth century Babylonian Targum *Targum Onkelos,* which drew many of its interpretations from the early Midrashim, including the *Midrash Sifre,* reflects the view of *Sifre*. Thus, in its translation of 22:29, for example, the ass is not said to criticize Balaam, "you have acted ruthlessly," but the translator softens the words to, "you have mocked me." This *Targum* also adds the concept of "prophecy" in 24:2 and elevates Balaam's role.

Midrash Pesikta d' Rabbi Kahana

The Midrash Pesikta d'Rabbi Kahana is also positive. It states that no philosophers rose among the nations of the world that equaled Balaam.

Middle path
Josephus

The first century Jewish historian Josephus wrote (in *Antiquities* 4, 6, 13, 158) that Balaam

> …was the man to whom Moses did the high honor of recording his prophecies; and though it was open to him to appropriate and take credit for them himself, as there would have been no witness to convict him [he piously refrained from doing so]…. His memory is perpetuated by the biblical story.

Balaam's fault, according to Josephus, was his misguided desire to please King Balak. Josephus calls Balaam "the greatest of the prophets at that time," a man who did not speak by "inspiration," but by "divine spirit." He went with Balak's messengers because he understood that this was God's will. When he learned through the episode of the ass that God was displeased with his journey, he decided to stop his journey and return home, but God told him to continue the trip. Balaam advised Balak how to corrupt the Israelite men with female prostitutes, yet, he warned Balak that the victory achieved through this scheme would only be a small misfortune and a temporary setback to the Israelites.

Summary

Contrary to the view of many Synagogue attendees, Judaism is not monolithic. Its sages can and do disagree, as shown in the variety of interpretations given to the Balaam story. Some of the sages felt that he was acting properly, some the reverse. Some were convinced that he was a great prophet, but that he handled the incident with the Israelites in a misguided manner. Others disagreed. They felt that Balaam was a dishonorable soothsayer.

Pinchas

Should we copy Pinchas' zealotry?

Chapter 25 of the book of *Numbers* narrates the story of Aaron's grandson Pinchas' zealous behavior. When the Israelites settled in Shittim, during their forty-year stay in the desert, many of them disobeyed God's command. They accepted the cunning invitation of the Moabites and Midianites who had invited them to participate in their feasts, idol worship and sexual escapades. This, they were certain, would lead them from God.

The Bible states that God reacted by launching a devastating plague and by instructing Moses to round up the leaders of the rebellion and hang them. Before the command could be implemented, one of the rebels, a tribal leader, in shocking and brazen disregard of God and Moses, carried a Midianite woman to the sacred Tent of Meeting and arrogantly had sex with her in public view.

While Moses and other Israelites looked on, immobilized by shock, Pinchas rose, grasped a spear and pierced the Israelite man and the Midianite woman, killing them both. Pinchas' act halted the plague, which had killed twenty-four thousand Israelites.

God spoke again to Moses, mentioned zealotry three times, and said, Pinchas "turned My wrath from the Israelites when he zealously avenged My zealousness among them, so I did not consume the Israelites in My zealousness."

Questions
1. Does God become angry?
2. Did Pinchas act correctly?
3. Should people be zealous for God?

God's wrath and zealousness are anthropopathisms: Metaphors ascribing human emotions to God

God, of course, is not human and has no human emotions. The term "My wrath" is not referring to God, who does not become angry, but to the plague. God is stating that Pinchas' act stopped the plague.

Zealousness means ardent activity. The Bible commentator Rashi (1040–1105) explains it as a short-hand way of describing one person's strong reaction to another. In this verse, God is not expressing an emotion, but explaining the consequences of the Israelites' immorality, the plague.

Overzealousness by people is wrong

The American patriarch Benjamin Franklin insisted that to be overzealous in religion is to be irreligious.

Ambrose Bierce, in his humorous but perceptive *The Devil's Dictionary* agreed. He considered zealousness an immature reaction of an inexperienced person who lacks judgment to act properly. He defined "zeal" as: "A certain nervous disorder affecting the young and inexperienced; a passion that goes before a fall."

Jim Coople agreed. God, he wrote, disapproves of such behavior because its after-effect is destruction.

> When Zeal sought Gratitude for his reward,
> He went away exclaiming: "O my Lord!"
> "What do you want?" the Lord asked, bending down.
> "An ointment for my cracked and bleeding crown."

There are all too many "religious" zealots in this world. More deaths have resulted from overly-zealous people and groups than any other cause. Yet, blind to this fact, and perceiving over-zealousness as piety, the number of over-zealous today numbers in the millions.

Was Pinchas overzealous?

The ancient Jewish commentators differed on whether Pinchas acted correctly. Certainly the Israelite leader was wrong in what he did before the Tent of Meeting and should have been stopped. But should he have been speared without a warning and a trial? Did the non-Israelite woman deserve to be killed?

Scripture states that God awarded Pinchas with "My covenant of peace." The rationalistic Bible commentator ibn Ezra (1089–1164) – apparently questioning the merit of Pinchas' action – down-plays the reward by explaining that this means that God is assuring Pinchas that he will not be avenged by the family of the man that he killed.

Rashi (1040–1105) had no qualms about Pinchas' behavior. God also handed Pinchas "a covenant of eternal priesthood," which Rashi states means that although Pinchas was not selected to be a priest when his grandfather Aaron was raised to that position, he was now elevated to that role.

The book of *Psalms* 106:28–31 retells the story of Pinchas and praises him, but the psalmist is careful not to call him a "zealot."

Later, many, but, of course, not all, rabbis disapproved of his zealotry. The fourth century Jerusalem Talmud, *Sanhedrin* 9:7, states that he transgressed the will of the sages. However, attempting to justify his behavior somewhat, the ninth century Aramaic translation of the bible called *Pseudo-Jonathan* rewrites the story by stating that Pinchas consulted with the court before acting.

In the early thirteenth century *Midrash Numbers Rabbah* 21:3 and the late third century *Genesis Rabbah* 21:5 and in many other sources, the rabbis identified Pinchas with the later zealous prophet Elijah because God's negative reaction to Elijah was clear. The Midrashim state that Pinchas lived a long life and in later centuries adopted the name Elijah. Elijah exhibited strong emotional zealous outbursts against the Israelites when he saw them ignoring God's commands. The sixth century Babylonian Talmud, *Baba Mezia* 85b, relates that Elijah was punished for his zeal with sixty flaming lashes. God told Elijah that He speaks in a "still small voice," meaning quietly, persuading, without emotional zeal. Then, seeing that Elijah would not be able to carry out his role properly, the *Midrash Song of Songs Rabbah* 1:6 (probably begun in the first half of the first millennium) states that God dismissed him and replaced him with a successor, the prophet Elisha. God took Elijah away "in a fiery chariot."

Summary

Pinchas, the grandson of Moses' brother Aaron and the future third high priest of Israel, saw an Israelite leader publicly and arrogantly rejecting God by committing a sexual act at the holy Tent of Meeting. He reacted with "zealousness" and killed the offender. God expresses His seeming approval and apparently rewards Pinchas. Yet the ancient rabbis questioned whether Pinchas acted properly. True, he stopped an offense, but, they asked, couldn't he have done it without killing the perpetrators? Wasn't he overzealous, and, therefore, wrong?

Robert E. Thompson described proper zeal: "All true zeal for God is zeal for love, mercy and goodness." Any other reason is wrong. "Nothing spoils human nature more than false zeal," wrote Benjamin Whichcote. And he continued: "The good nature of a heathen is more God-like than the furious zeal of a supposedly religious zealot."

Mattot

The power of speech

Numbers 30:3 contains God's command, "A man who vows a vow to the Lord or swears an oath, to bind himself with a binding obligation, *lo yachel* his word; he should do all that goes out of his mouth."

Questions
1. How did the ancients evaluate speech?
2. Can one swear to a truth?
3. It is more effective to learn by speaking or by reading?

Targum Onkelos
When *Genesis* 2:7 states that God blew into man's nostrils "the spirit of life," the ancient Aramaic translation of the Bible *Targum Onkelos* explains it as "the power of speech." This is a divine gift. It is the power that distinguishes humans from all other creations. It is the foundation upon which intelligence is built.

Humans were given a divine power. The significance of speech was recognized by all cultures. The Bible describes God creating the world through speech. The Egyptian goddess Isis is described as being "great" in *The Legend of Ra and Isis* because she had "the knowledge of words."

A false oath
The twelfth century rational Bible and Talmud commentator Rashbam translates the reading *lo yachel (Numbers* 30:3) as "do not delay to carry it out," when the command is restated in the *Deuteronomy* 23:22 version of the command.

However the earlier fifth century *Midrash Sifre* focuses on another meaning of *yachel,* "to make profane." It stresses the importance, indeed the sanctity, of speech, and renders it "do not desecrate." It pictures the person who violates his vow as a person who defiles a holy object.

The Babylonian Talmud, *Shavuot* 39a, emphasized the punishment for a false oath:

> The whole world trembled at the time when the Holy One, blessed be He, said at Sinai: "Thou shalt not take the name of the Lord thy God in vain." And it is of such a transgressor that the Torah says "The Lord will not hold him guiltless," meaning, will not leave him unpunished. And moreover, for all other transgressions of the Torah, the sinner alone is punished, but in this case he and his family [are punished; meaning that the false oath generally effects other family members, and that when this occurs, the others suffer the same consequences].

Swearing to a truth

The twelfth century *Midrash Numbers Rabbah* even warns people not to swear truthfully. "If a man says to his friend: 'I swear that I will go and eat a certain food at a certain place'....and even fulfills the oath, he will be destroyed. If this happens to one who swears truthfully, the consequences to one who swears falsely will be so much greater!"

The *Midrash* proves its point with an example. Alexander Yannai, a Hasmonean king around 126–76 B.C.E., lost two thousand of his towns because he swore a true oath.

The *Midrash* states that people are only allowed to swear a true oath when three almost impossible conditions exist: (1) He must be as righteous as Abraham, Job and Joseph. (2) He must devote all of his time to the study of Torah and the performance of its laws. (3) He must marry his daughter to a student who spends all of his time studying Torah and support him financially so that he does not have to neglect his studies.

Swearing in court

The awe that some people have for the significance of an oath, whether true or false, has prompted them to avoid swearing altogether, even in court. Thus, many civilized countries today allow people who have such scruples to "affirm" rather than swear whenever a judicial oath is required.

Misusing words

In the fifth century before the Common Era, a group of Greek teachers called Sophists taught that the best skill for a person is rhetorics, the ability to use words to persuade others.

The Greek philosopher Plato, born in 427 B.C.E., railed against their practice with great fervor in many of his books. He stressed that the Sophists were teaching people to tell lies to gain their end, without any concern for the truth or proper behavior, which should be the goal of education.

In many instances, the need for an oath shows that something is wrong. For example, people frequently lie to procrastinate. Instead of swearing "I promise to do it," they should just do it.

The Greek satirist Lucian (c. 120–190 C.E.) wrote in his book *Hippias* (in the Loeb Classical Library translation): "Among wise men, I maintain, the most praiseworthy are they who not only have spoken cleverly on their particular subjects, but have made their assertions good by doing things to match them."

The power of speech over the written word

Plato also wrote that speech is more powerful than the written word.

In his book *Phaedrus,* he tells the myth of one god who visited another god to show him his new invention, letters. He told the other god that letters will improve people's memory and will make them wiser. The god was not impressed. He told the inventor that he thinks that the letters will have the opposite result. They will create forgetfulness because people will rely on the written words and not practice using their memory. Furthermore, those who learn only though reading, without discussing what they have read with another, will not fully understand what they are reading. Thus a well-read individual can not be wise; he only appears so.

Writing, Plato explains, is like a painting. The people in a painting may look like humans, but if one asks them a question, they remain silent. It is the same with the written word. One may think that what he reads is intelligent, but if he asks the page a question, he gets no response. The page is like a parrot, it continues to repeat the same words without answering questions. But when one talks with others and asks them a question, one is prompted to think and evaluate the answer.

Jewish tradition recognized the value of speaking with another during study and developed the *chavruta* method. In *chavruta*, two students study the Bible or Talmud text together, with each having ample opportunity to articulate the ideas in the text and to ask the other about it.

Summary

The Bible stresses the sanctity of speech. It is a gift from God that must not be abused. It is the element that distinguishes humans from all other creatures.

The Bible mandates that people should not profane words by promising or swearing to do something. This seems to refer to a false oath. However, many ancient sages see the Bible also prohibiting an oath even when the oath is true, except for required testimony in the court of law.

Speech is a more effective learning tool than the written word. When a person wants to learn and understand a subject, they would do better by discussing the lesson with another person rather than simply reading it.

Masei

When is Passover?

The question "When is Passover?" seems as simple as the humorous question, "Who is buried in Grant's tomb?" Everyone with the slightest bit of Jewish education would answer that it begins on the 15th day of the Jewish month of Nissan and ends seven days later in Israel or eight days later in the Diaspora. This is true today, but it was not always so. Indeed the holiday of Passover that is mentioned in the Bible occurs on the fourteenth of Nissan and last only a single day.

Questions
1. What is the difference between Passover and *Chag Hamatzot?*
2. When did Jews stop observing Passover?

Passover and *Chag Hamatzot*
The spring holiday of Passover, as it is practiced today, commemorates the deliverance of the Israelites through Moses' leadership from the hardship of Egyptian slavery and their exodus from Egypt. It also celebrates the later spring barley harvest in Israel. The name comes from the tenth plague, when God "passed over" (or, "protected") the Israelite dwellings when he slew the firstborn of Egypt. The holiday is called *Chag Hamatzot*, the festival of the unleavened bread, and not Passover, as in the Siddur, the Jewish prayer book, and in other rabbinical texts.

While this is the same holiday today, Passover and *Chag Hamatzot* were two very distinct holidays in the Bible; although the Bible explains that both commemorate the exodus from Egypt.

The Passover celebration, as indicated in *Leviticus* 23:5 and *Numbers* 28:16, began on the day of the fourteenth of Nissan and lasted until the morning of the fifteenth. The Israelites were required to offer a sacrifice, called the Passover or Pascal lamb, on the fourteenth and eat it in family groups that night (the beginning of the fifteenth of Nissan – because the Jewish practice is that the day begins the evening before). *Chag Hamatzot* began on that same evening of the fifteenth and partially overlapped the Passover: the two shared the night of the fifteenth, but not the day of the fourteenth. Thus the children probably asked "Why is this night different than all other nights since we are celebrating two holidays at the same time?"

The end of the Pascal sacrifice

The biblical Passover, as we noted, was entirely associated with the Pascal sacrifice. When the first and second Temples were constructed, it was brought in the Temple, for no sacrifice could be offered outside of the Temple. The historian Josephus relates in his book *Wars* that over three million Jews gathered in Jerusalem to perform the sacrifice in 65 C.E. The Babylonian Talmud, *Pessachim* 64b, tells that King Agrippa took a census of the people about this time by counting the kidneys of the sacrificed lambs. There were over a million kidneys, meaning that over a million Jewish families participated in the sacrifice.

When the Temple was destroyed by invading Roman forces in the year 70 of the Common Era, Jews felt that they could not make an exception and continue the Pascal sacrifice outside the destroyed Temple. Thus the practice of the biblical Passover ceased and nothing replaced it on the fourteenth of Nissan. Some Jews may have continued the sacrifices in some modified form for a short period, but they did not persist in doing so for long.

Shocked at the cessation of the biblically mandated Pascal sacrifice by the Jews, the Samaritans, a quasi-Jewish sect, insisted that the sacrifice must not stop, and so they still bring the Pascal sacrifice even today on Mount Gerizim near Shechem in Israel.

Renaming *Chag Hamatzot*

Unwilling to cede the Romans a victory over their religious practices, the Jews, who discontinued the sacrifice, began to call *Chag Hamatzot* by the name of Passover. Nevertheless, they were careful to retain the original name Chag Hamatzot in the prayer book and other rabbinical texts.

This history was recognized by most Bible commentators. *Numbers* 33:3 recalls the exodus and states: "They [the Israelites] traveled from Ramses during the first month [Nissan], on the fifteenth day of the first month, on *the day following* the Passover…."

Ibn Ezra (1089–1164) comments on this verse and writes that he explained that Passover occurred on the fourteenth of Nissan in his commentary to *Leviticus* 23:11. Chizkunee, in his comment on this verse and on *Leviticus* 23:8, states that the fourteenth was named Passover because the Pascal sacrifice was brought on that day. He proves this by referring to what Scripture states in *Leviticus* 23:5 and 8 and *Numbers* 28:16 and 17. These verses state clearly that the fourteenth of Nissan is Passover and the fifteenth begins the seven days of *Chag Hamatzot*.

Summary

As surprising as it may appear and as opposite as it is to the common conception of the Passover holiday, the recognition of the distinction between Passover and *Chag Hamatzot* is the "traditional interpretation" of the biblical text. The first was a Temple-oriented holiday that occurred on the fourteenth of Nissan; the second began on the fifteenth and continued for seven days. When the Pascal lamb sacrifice, the central practice of Passover ceased with the destruction of the second Temple, the Jews labeled *Chag Hamatzot* by the name Passover. However, the holiday is still called by its ancient biblical name in the prayer book.

Devarim

Did God or Moses write the book of *Deuteronomy?*

Bible critics, as is well known, insist that neither God nor Moses wrote *Deuteronomy*. Many of them contend that the essence of the Book originated during the first Temple period in the reign of King Josiah (640–609 B.C.E.) and that it was placed in its final form during the early second Temple period by Ezra the Scribe.

Questions
1. What are the "traditional" views of the rabbis and Bible sages concerning the author of *Deuteronomy?*
2. If we believe that Moses wrote the book without a divine command, is it still holy?

Different views on the authorship of *Deuteronomy*
Talmud, Zohar and Maharal of Prague
Contrary to the common belief that the entire Pentateuch was dictated by God to Moses, traditional scholars have different answers to this question.

The Babylonian Talmud, *Megillah* 31b, notes that both the biblical books of *Leviticus* and *Deuteronomy* contain lists of curses that will plague the Israelites if they fail to observe God's commands, but the former addresses the Israelites in the plural, while the latter uses the singular. The Talmud concludes that God dictated the former to Moses, while Moses uttered the latter on his own initiative.

The Babylonian Talmud, *Bava Bathra* 88b, also recognized that Moses composed the curses in *Deuteronomy*. It contrasted his human articulation with the better composition by God and concludes that God is different than humans. God blessed the Israelites with twenty-two letters and cursed them with eight. Moses reversed the numbers. He blessed them with eight and cursed them with twenty-two.

The thirteenth century *Zohar* to *Vaethanan* agrees, "*Deuteronomy* was said by Moses himself." It is "the oral law," since it originated with Moses who was explaining the first four books.

Rabbi Judah Loew, known as the Maharal of Prague (around 1512–1609), in his *Tipheret Yisrael*, also admits that *Deuteronomy* contains Moses' opinions.

Abraham ibn Ezra

The rational Bible commentator Ibn Ezra (1089–1164), believed that some parts of Scripture could not have been written by Moses because the events occurred after his death. He wrote that the post-Moses author(s) composed what they wrote with "divine prophecy."

Critics have understood for a long time that ibn Ezra was a "radical." Some claim that he only hints at his radical views, criticizes the radical ideas of others but reports them at great length because he secretly believed them and wanted to publicize them, and adds statements such as "but it was done with divine prophecy," even though he did not believe it, to deceive his general readership and protect himself from criticism and censor.

Ibn Ezra does not explicitly address the issue of the origin of *Deuteronomy* as a whole. He writes in his commentary to the Ten Commandments that the *Exodus* version was the original divine version of the Decalogue and the text in *Deuteronomy*, which differs in many respects from *Exodus* and has additions, is Moses' "explanation" of the Decalogue. This could suggest that Moses wrote not only the Decalogue and the other sections that ibn Ezra specifically identifies, but also more of *Deuteronomy*.

Nachmanides

The mystic Nachmanides (1195–1270) had a somewhat similar idea. In his commentary to the beginning of *Deuteronomy*, Nachmanides divides the book of *Deuteronomy* into three parts. The first contains words of reproof; the end has blessings, curses and a song; while the middle and largest section is a recapitulation and elaboration of the statutes and ordinances. Nachmanides states that when Moses is instructing the Israelites with new previously unmentioned laws, he is stating words as commanded by God. However, when he repeats and explains laws, or otherwise gives his opinion on matters, he is presenting his own view. Thus, he accepts the notion that at least the greater part of *Deuteronomy* contains Moses' own vision of Israelite history and the laws in the prior four Pentateuchal volumes. Nachmanides adds a new notion: that Moses had no intention of recording his explanations until God told him to write them in *Deuteronomy*.

As C. B. Chavel translates the words of Nachmanides:

> Moses wished to explain the Torah to them [the Israelites]. This is said to inform us that Moses saw fit to do so although God had not commanded him thereon [but afterwards when He commanded him to write down the entire Torah, God Himself said all these words that were originally spoken by Moses; and Moses wrote them as He commanded. Hence there is no difference between the first four books of the Torah and the fifth book, *Deuteronomy*, as all are equally the word of God].

Isaac Caro

Isaac ben Joseph Caro, a Spanish scholar who was expelled from Spain in 1492, addressed this question in his book *Toledot Yitzhak*. He points out that the *Mishnah Sanhedrin* and the discussion in the Babylonian Talmud, *Sanhedrin* 99a, seem to contradict the view that Moses wrote the book of *Deuteronomy*, or at least parts of it on his own initiative. He explains that, despite appearances, these sources do not contradict this idea.

The *Mishnah* states: "The following have no portion [in the world to come]….He who maintains that…the Torah was not divinely revealed." The Talmud elaborates: "And even if he asserts that the entire Torah is from heaven, except for a particular verse, which [he insists] was not uttered by God but by Moses [he is deprived of the world to come]."

Caro answers the seeming inconsistency between this talmudic statement and the opinions that we previously quoted by saying that the position in *Sanhedrin* only applies to the first four Pentateuchal books. But, he continues, *Deuteronomy*, as Nachmanides states, contains Moses' thoughts, which after Moses had expressed them, God told Moses to record in the Torah.

Don Isaac Abravanel

Caro's contemporary Don Isaac Abravanel (1437–1508) disagreed. He contented that every word of the Torah, including *Deuteronomy*, "comes from the mouth of the Almighty: God commanded that it be written word for word."

Summary

There are different answers to the question: did God or Moses write the book of *Deuteronomy*? The points of view differ widely, from one extreme to another, with a spectrum of opinions in between. What must be remembered, however, is that even if we assume that parts or all of *Deuteronomy* was written by Moses without a divine command, this does not detract from its sanctity. For the wisdom of the Torah was inspired by God. Besides, even the rabbis who felt that Moses wrote his own ideas in *Deuteronomy* stated that he was explaining what God had commanded.

Va'etchanan

Do we need commentaries to understand the Bible?

It is absolutely impossible to understand the Bible without at least two or three first-class commentaries.

Questions
1. Why are translations inadequate without commentaries in explaining the Bible?
2. How do the words of the *shema* exemplify this deficiency?

Translations are not enough
While it is true that a translation is an explanation of the text, and hence to some degree a commentary, the nature of a translation which requires brevity and discourages elaboration, makes it insufficient to fully explain the text.

The *shema* is a good example
This difficulty can be seen if we examine one of the most well-known, but least understood sections of Scripture, *Deuteronomy* 6:4–9. This section contains the *shema,* which is recited by many Jews as many as three times a day, as an affirmation of their relation to God. The first two verses are translated in the 1955 version of The Jewish Publication Society as follows.

> Hear, O Israel: the Lord our God, the Lord is one. And thou shalt love the Lord thy God with all thy heart, and with all thy soul, and with all thy might.

On one level, the text can be understood as translated. However a closer analysis of the words reveals a different level of understanding.

The introductory verb *shema*

The first word *shema* is translated "hear." It is true that *shema* literally means "hear"; however, it should be obvious that God wants the Israelites to do more than use their sense of hearing. The term "hear" is also used as a figure of speech for "accept" both in Hebrew and in English. When one says to another "hear me and do what I say," he means "accept my view and do what I am telling you." The command *shema* also has this figurative meaning, God wants the people to not only listen but accept what He is about to say. This is how the decree is translated by the Aramaic translation *Targum Pseudo-Jonathan* (written, according to some authorities, around the eight century of the Common Era).

O

The exclamation "O" in the JPS translation is generally understood as solemn and poetic language designed to lend earnestness to an appeal. Is "O" in the Hebrew? It is not. The JPS translators and the many others that use the "O" apparently felt that this command was so solemn they ought to highlight it with the "O." Tradition, as we will see, agrees that the command is important, but we also need to understand that this highlighting is not in the Hebrew original.

Israel

The word *shema* is written in the singular while the phrase "our (God)" is in the plural. How should the mandate be understood? Is "Israel" the people as a whole, without any individual responsibility, or is the name directed to each individual? The consensus among the rabbinical interpreters is that it is an individual responsibility.

The Lord

The name "Lord," used twice in this sentence, does not appear in the Hebrew. The Hebrew uses the Tetragrammaton, four letters without vowels that represent the "ineffable name" of God. It is commonly transliterated in English as "Jehovah." Jews felt that they must not pronounce the name outside of the Temple. When Egyptian Jewry made the first Bible translation, rendering it into Greek, they sidestepped the problem of using the Tetragrammaton by substituting a Greek word meaning "Lord." This practice was continued in the JPS and other English translations.

Our God

The Hebrew language does not have the verb "is." Should the verse be translated "Hear O Israel, the Lord **is** our God, the Lord is one." This would direct us to accept the Lord as God **and** know that He is one. Without "is," the passage requires us only to know that He is one. The JPS translation, as we saw, took the second approach. This is the view of Maimonides (1138–1204) who reasoned that "accepting" God has no meaning. It does not state what act is required. If it implies belief, one can not mandate belief, either one believes or not – it can not be forced. Maimonides sees the command regarding our relationship to God in the first word of the next verse.

(is) One

The following word is "one." We are told to know that the Lord is one. This is an obscure thought requiring interpretation. Are we instructed to know that there is no other God but the "Lord" or is the injunction to understand that God's "oneness" is unique, unlike any other kind of oneness? Maimonides takes the latter stance. In short, he understands this verse to state that one must study and know that God's oneness is unique. He considers it the second of the 613 commandments in his *Book of Commandments* and discusses it in detail in his *Mishneh Torah, Hilchot Yesodei Hatorah* 1:7.

The second verse of the *shema:* "And thou shalt love the Lord thy God"

As much as the first verse demonstrates the need for commentary, the following verse demands this even more. Maimonides observes that it is not realistic to suppose that one can require another to love anything, even God. Thus, he argues, that the phrase "love God" must mean something else. He identifies this something else as the mandate to use one's intelligence, study nature, develop an understanding of the world, and know God as much as one is able to do so. He starts his *Hilchot Yesodei Hatorah* with these words:

> The basic principle and pillar of wisdom is to know that there is a
> primary entity that brought about all that exists. Everything that exists,

from heaven to earth and all in between, does not exist other than through the truth of His existence.

Heart

How strong is the injunction to "know"? *Deuteronomy* tells us "with all thy heart, and with all thy soul, and with all thy might." These words seem simple. The problem is that a good commentary will point out that the Hebrew does not say what this translation leads us to believe it says.

The word "heart" is commonly thought today to suggest the seat of emotions. Thus the verse would be directing us to direct all our emotions to God. We have already found that this is unreasonable; one can not order another to love. The answer is that the "heart" in the Bible was considered in all verses in which it appears as the seat of the intellect. As in *Proverbs* 15:14, "A discerning heart [mind] seeks knowledge." Similarly, when God is said to harden Pharaoh's heart (in *Exodus* 7:3 and other passages), He is hardening his thoughts. In the Bible, the kidney is considered the site of affection, as in *Jeremiah* 11:20, 17:10, and 20:12. Thus, the first part of the instruction is to study, learn, know and use our entire mind.

Soul, or is it body

Similarly, the word *nefesh*, which means "soul" in modern Hebrew, and is rendered so in the JPS translation, never has this meaning in the Bible. It means one's body, one's being or one's life. In this verse, it means we should know God and demonstrate our knowledge of Him with our entire being. Rashi (1040–1105) and his grandson, the twelfth century French Bible commentator Rashbam, accepted the view of the second century rabbi Akiva, "with your life," meaning being willing to give up your life. This extreme view was rejected by the twelfth century Spanish Bible commentator Abraham ibn Ezra who understood it to mean "with your entire kidney [all your desires]." This view is contrary to that of Maimonides.

Might

The final requirement in this verse *m'odecha,* which is translated by JPS "with all thy might," is, quite frankly obscure. One can only guess or rely on a reliable commentator for its meaning. Rashi offers two choices, the first from the

Talmud and the authoritative fourth century translation of Aramaic *Targum Onkelos*. The second is from a Midrash. The first is "possessions," meaning one must be willing to give up his possessions for God. The second is "accept whatever God dishes out to you, whether good or bad." Ibn Ezra and the thirteenth century French Bible commentator Chizkunee see *m'odecha* as not being a new command, but a charge to do the prior two acts with as much power as you can muster.

Summary

A study of the well-known *shema* shows that there is virtually no word in the two verses that we discussed that can be understood without two or three good Bible commentaries. And then the readers, students or persons reading the verses need to decide which view they feel they can accept.

Eikev

Should we act to get a reward?

The biblical portion of *Eikev*, beginning with *Deuteronomy* 7:12, details the rewards that one can expect to receive for obeying God's laws. The second paragraph of the *shema, Deuteronomy* 11:13–21, which is recited twice daily by observant Jews, also contains promised incentives. There are many other similar biblical sections. In *Deuteronomy* 7, the gains will be children, fruit, grain, wine, oil, cattle, flocks, goats, no infertility, no illnesses and no enemies. In *Deuteronomy* 11, it is rain, grain, wine, oil, and grass for animals. Both of these portions and the others include a list of punishments that will follow the failure to observe the commands. It appears that most people, Jews and non-Jews, obey God's laws because they are motivated by reward and punishment.

Questions
1. Should one obey divine laws because he will be rewarded for doing so and punished if he fails to do so?
2. Are extrinsic payments, such as those listed above, the only benefit one can expect from proper behavior?
3. Is it possible that the world is so constructed by God that good behavior is its own reward?
4. Is the expectation of reward and punishment a childish idea?
5. Could it be that Scripture speaks of reward and punishment because this is the only way to stimulate most people to act properly?
6. Do all people agree on the answers to these questions?

Various opinions
There are vast disagreements with passionate feelings over this issue.

Mishnahs

The *Mishnah Avot* 1:3 contends that one should not depend on reward and punishment. Antigonos of Socho states: "Be not like the servant who serves a master on the condition of receiving a gift; but be like the servant who serves a master not on the condition of receiving an award." The *Mishnah Avot d'Rabbi Natan* reports that Antigonos' position provoked strong disagreement. It repeats the statement and elaborates that Antigonos' two disciples, Zadok and Boethos, rebuffed his teaching and lapsed into heresy. They were stunned, "Is it conceivable that a laborer works all day and does not take his pay home in the evening?"

Maimonides

Moses Maimonides (1138–1204) spoke against the reliance on reward and punishment in his introduction to the tenth chapter of the talmudic tractate of *Sanhedrin, Chelek.* "There are many different opinions, but these are based on differences in understanding." Some people believe that after death they will enjoy physically delightful rewards in the Garden of Eden if they are righteous and the fiery flames of Gehinnom if they sin. Others think that the righteous will receive payment in the era of the Messiah when their bodies will be perfected and they will live like kings forever; while those who were evil will not live at that time. A third group is convinced that the ultimate happiness for the righteous is the resurrection of the dead, including the reuniting of families. A fourth approach is that reward and punishment is given in this material world in the form of bodily pleasures and worldly achievements. A fifth position, the most popular, combines the various ideas: the Messiah will come, he will resurrect the dead, we will enter the Garden of Eden, "where we will eat and drink in health forever." Some call this fifth approach "the world to come."

Maimonides rejected all five positions. He considered them to be immature and childish. People who rely on rewards and punishments are like the child who is taken to school for the first time and is only motivated to learn by being bribed with candies. As he grows older and outgrows candies, the bribe is upgraded to shoes and other clothes. When he is still older, the bribe is money. Then, when he "matures," he is encouraged to learn so that he will be "a rabbi or a judge and others will honor you." "All this," says Maimonides, "is shameful. It is only necessary because of the immature nature of people who need bribes. They make the ultimate goal of study something other than the study itself." The ultimate purpose of study should be knowledge, to know what is true.

Maimonides quotes Antigonos to support his view as well as other talmudic and midrashic statements. The *Midrash Sifre on Deuteronomy* 11:13 states: "Should a person say: I will study Torah so that I will become wealthy… so that I will be called 'rabbi,'… so that I will receive payment in the world to come. Behold, it is written: 'to love your God.' Everything that you do, do only out of love."

Maimonides contends that people are encouraged to believe in reward and punishment until they are sufficiently intellectually mature to understand the truth and stop insisting on bribes like the immature child. The truth is what the sages taught in *Avot:* do not observe the *mitzvot shelo lishmah*: "not for the sake [of the Torah] itself." The ultimate benefit for observing God's commands, like the ultimate reward for study, is the natural consequences of the deed itself. In regard to study it is the gaining of knowledge and truth. In regard to other behavior it is the performance of that which is right. Maimonides speaks on these issues at length, with many examples, and it is well worth one's time to read his work *Chelek*.

Rashbatz

Rabbi Shimon ben Tzemach Duran (known as Rashbatz, 1361–1444) agreed with Maimonides. He explained that there are conflicting rabbinical statements on the subject because most people have not reached Maimonides' level of maturity and need assurances that they will be compensated for acting properly. Professor Yeshayahu Leibowitz (1904–1994) supported the Maimonidean attitude so strongly that he repeats a teaching by him in almost every one of his books. The first paragraph of the daily recited *shema, Deuteronomy* 5:4–9, does not mention reward and punishment. It reflects the mature perception. The second paragraph, *Deuteronomy* 11:13–21, which mentions these promises, is the presentation for the masses of people.

Don Isaac Abravanel

Needless to say many people disagreed with the Maimonidean view and his interpretation of the Talmud and Midrash. He was viciously vilified in his own lifetime for his ideas. An example of disagreement is Don Isaac Abravanel (1437–1508). In his commentary to *Avot*, he argues that Antigonos is simply wrong. It is human nature that people expect to be paid for meritorious acts. Antigonos used a servant as an example; most servants work for wages. He rejects the Maimonidean concept that one should act properly only because of the intrinsic significance of the deed: that the benefit of a *mitzvah* is the performance of the *mitzvah*. He claims that there is no Rabbinic source supporting his position. He criticizes Maimonides for relying on the teaching of the non-Jewish philosopher Aristotle for his stance. He sees no intrinsic value in commands such as *tzitzit, tefillin* and *mezuzah*. They should be performed with an eye toward an after-life recompense. When the rabbis said that the compensation for a *mitzvah* is the *mitzvah*, they meant that some commands have intrinsic benefits in addition to those gained after death.

Summary

As with virtually all matters of Jewish belief, the rabbis take various sides on whether there is reward and punishment after life. Scripture itself promises these items repeatedly. So, too, do the majority of Rabbinic statements in the Talmuds, Midrashim and other writings. However, there are other perspectives that say that the statements made in these sources were made for the masses of people who are insufficiently mature to live their lives properly without the bribe of a reward and punishment.

We saw the statement of Antigonos that one should not expect payment. We saw also the talmudic view that the true compensation for a *mitzvah* is the intrinsic value of the *mitzvah* itself. We also saw that even among those that expect recompense in the after-life, their description of what this is differs radically. Maimonides lists five different notions on the subjects and rejects them all as childish.

All of the commentators, including Maimonides, agree that one may believe in reward and punishment, although some, as Maimonides, feel that one should work to mature and discard the notion.

R'eih

The "sin of useless action"

Before the Israelites entered the land of Canaan, the land that would be called Israel, God warned them in *Deuteronomy* 12. They must utterly destroy every vestige of Canaanite idol worship. If they did so, they would have no problems with the enemies around them. If they did not, they would suffer.

Questions

1. Is the eradication of idolatry a basic object of the Torah?
2. Is the sin of idolatry relevant today?

Maimonides

In the *Guide of the Perplexed* 3:29, Maimonides (1138–1204) states: "it is the *principle object of the law* and the axis around which it turns, to eradicate these opinions [idolatry] from the human heart and make the existence of idolatry impossible." "Those who reject idolatry," he continues, "follow, as it were, the entire law." In 3:30, he resumes and stresses, "God, showing us mercy, wanted to remove this error from our minds… and therefore He wanted us to discontinue the practice of *these useless actions*."

The phrase "useless actions" is thought provoking. Is idolatry wrong because it produces "useless actions"? Or is the reverse true, since idolatry is wrong it is useless?

It would be interesting to speculate that idolatry is forbidden because it is useless, because it has no value, and because humans have a duty to undertake useful actions, such as to better themselves and society. This approach would answer three questions: (1) What is basic about idolatry that makes its eradication "a principle object of the law"? (2) Isn't calling idolatry a "principle object of the law" in conflict with Maimonides' statement in 3:30 that the purpose of biblical laws is to teach some truths *and* to improve society and individuals? (3) Since idolatry is no longer common, doesn't it appear that the "principle object of the law" is no longer relevant?

The mandate to perform useful acts

In regard to the first question, it is possible that idolatry and everything like it is forbidden because it is useless. The law forbidding idolatry is a basic principle underlining not only of the law but also of humanity. People are required to perform certain useful acts, such as learn about the world and God, and use this knowledge to be all that they can be and to improve society. One who spends his time in useless behavior is violating the basic duty of a human being and is acting like an unthinking and non-acting non-human.

In response to the second question, seeing the avoidance of useless behavior as a basic principle does not negate the fact that the purpose of biblical law is to teach some truths **and** to improve society and the individual. The concept of avoiding useless behavior, as we said, prompts us to work to develop our minds and improve individual and societal behavior.

Replying to the question whether the laws of idolatry is relevant, it is certainly generally true that idolatry is not prevalent. However this does not mean that the underpinning of this basic principle is no longer relevant. Unfortunately, all too many humans are still involved in useless behavior.

Summary

Thus, before entering the land of Canaan, the land that would be called Israel and the land that is symbolic of our entering a better world, *Deuteronomy* 12 mandated that we eradicate all vestiges of useless behavior and devote ourselves to what is useful. If we do so, God will remove all enemies around us. We will develop ourselves and this will make it possible for us to live properly and securely. If we fail to do so, we will not enter the Promised Land even if we complacently think that we are living there.

Shoftim

The power of the royal

The biblical portion *Shoftim* includes the laws of kings. The royal power brings to mind the ridiculous belief once held by many people, and still held today by some who don't know they are retaining this ancient idea. It is the notion of the healing power of the king's hand. It is based on the conviction that the king was a divine appointee and, hence, carried some divine strength, including the ability to heal.

Question
1. What did the ancients believe about the power of the king and how is it still believed today?

Ambrose Bierce
The nineteenth century American satirist Ambrose Bierce wrote in his *The Devil's Dictionary,* "'the most pious Edward' [king] of England used to lay his royal hand upon his ailing subjects and make them whole."

Bierce continued, "The superstition that maladies can be cured by royal taction is dead, but like many a departed conviction it has left a monument of custom to keep its memory green. The practice of forming in line and shaking the president's hand had no other origin, and when that great dignitary bestows his healing salutation on… visiting people… [they] are handing along an extinguished torch which once was kindled at the altar-fire of a faith long held by all classes of men."

What other "monuments of custom" has this superstition left as our legacy?
Dare we pause and consider the underlying rationale for our desire to press hands with clergy at the conclusion of services? Is there some semblance between these clergy and the preacher who panders to the pitiful masses who

seek the healing from he who declares that he can touch and cure his flock though the medium of television waves? Dare we ask if we are seeking some cure or spiritual elevation or are only performing a friendly social act?

Are those who kiss the Torah scroll as it passes them on its way to the platform or ark, or who kiss the holy book when they close it, showing a sign of affection and respect or something more? When a father blesses his child on Friday evening, is his blessing more effective because he, as *pater familias*, touched his child?

Is it wrong to have such beliefs? It is if one relinquishes control over one's life and relies on superstition.

$$* \quad * \quad *$$

Is it good to have a king?

The ancients disagreed whether it is good to have a king with supreme and absolute power to rule over Israel. *Deuteronomy* 17:14–20 contains a positive command to establish a monarchy. Yet, the prophet Samuel railed against it in *I Samuel* 8:4–22. He recited a long list showing how royal rule involves the sacrifice of personal freedoms: people give over the power that they should have over their lives to someone who is interested in his own agenda. Don Isaac Abravanel (1437–1508) agreed that monarchy is wrong. He was a court official and Bible commentator who saw with his own eyes how the king and queen of Spain abused their royal power and expelled Jews in 1492.

The rabbis analyzed the question and were bothered by the conflict that they saw in Jewish history. They held the conviction that the monarchy belonged only to the descendants of King David, but saw that many Jewish kings were not related to David. The kings of the northern kingdom of Israel were not of his house, yet some of them were appointed to the throne by prophets. This seemed to imply divine approval and authenticity to non-Davidic kings. Furthermore, the Hasmonean kings were not Davidic.

The rabbis resolved their quandary somewhat as follows. They acknowledged that there is a biblical command to have a king. They stated that Samuel did not disagree with the clear biblical statement. They explained his opposition to his conviction that the people of his generation were demanding a king for the wrong reason. They were acting in a contentious manner with a primary improper goal of ridding themselves of the prophetic authority of

Samuel. The rabbis recognized the legitimacy of only those kings of the north who were appointed by a prophet and who later showed they were worthy to hold the throne. Thus they dismissed the legitimacy of all the Hasmonean kings and most of those who held the northern throne. The true king in their view was Davidic, with very few exceptions when God saw the need and because of the exigencies of the moment.

The rabbinical view was incorporated into the Synagogue liturgy with prayers being recited daily for the restoration of the Davidic dynasty, including statements that the Messiah would be from this royal line.

Despite the recognition of the biblical command and the general Rabbinic desire for a Davidic king, the Bible and later Rabbinic writings retained the fear expressed by Samuel and set restraints upon the royal power, so that Judaism could assure that the king does not abuse his power.

Summary

There are conflicting views, pro and con, whether it is good for Jews to have a king. The underlying fear was that the king would abuse his power. A second and to some a primary concern was that Judaism feels that royalty belongs only to the Davidic family. A third worry is the giving up of personal powers and an over reliance, perhaps even a superstitious reliance, on royal power.

Ki Teitzei

Accept the truth no matter what its source

After devoting three chapters in the book of *Numbers* with ninety-six verses to the story of the non-Israelite prophet Balaam, Scripture adds another two verses In *Deuteronomy* 23:5–6 to remind us that God refused to listen to Balaam and turned his planned curses into blessings.

Questions
1. Why did the Bible allocate so many verses to the non-Israelite?
2. Should we pay attention to non-Jewish views?

Maimonides' opinion
In his Introduction to his *Shemoneh Perakim*, Maimonides states that he will be explaining the *Mishnah Pirke Avot* with ideas derived from ancient Jewish sages, Midrashim, the Talmuds and many other sources, including the works of non-Jewish philosophers of early and later generations, and many other texts. He warns his readers not to dismiss the ideas of non-Jews simply because they were written by non-Jews. We must "accept the truth no matter what its source." He repeats the same concept with more details when he discusses the science of astronomy in his code of Jewish laws, *Mishneh Torah, Hilchot Kiddush Hachodesh* 17:24. He acknowledges there that he derived his understanding of "the wisdom of astronomy and geometry" from books written by the ancient Greeks. "But since all of these ideas are subject to clear proofs, leaving no room for doubt, one should not concern himself about the author's identity, whether the idea was composed by a prophet or a non-Jew. When anything is rational and obviously true, pay no attention to the individual who made the statement or taught the idea, but to the proofs and reasons that he presented."

The attitude of Nehama Leibowitz

Maimonides was not the only scholar who accepted the truth when the source was not Jewish. There were many.

The Yeshivat Chovevei Torah Rabbinical School Journal of 2005 relates the famed twentieth century scholar Nehama Leibowitz's response to those who criticized her for including non-Jewish views in her Torah commentaries. She wrote: "It is true that I cite the words of people who are not observant of the *mitzvot*, if their words seem correct to me, and can reveal the light of Torah and display its greatness and holiness to the student. [I work] according to [Maimonides'] principle: "Accept the truth from wherever it comes." She cites the "extreme Reformer" and "anti-Zionist" Benno Jacob as an example. She learned "from his books... more than from many books written by bona-fide God-fearing Jews.... Several times, I showed *talmidei hakhamim* [Talmud scholars] details from Benno Jacob's important book *Auge um Auge* and they thanked me and rejoiced as if discovering a great treasure. Should I hide the name of the author? This I can not do."

She states that "even Abravanel [the fifteenth century sage who was driven from Spain with the other Jews in 1492 because they would not convert to the Catholic faith] in select places quotes the words of a Catholic bishop, and accepts his opinion over the opinions of [the traditional rabbis] Radak and Ralbag."

The judgment of Baruch Epstein

Another twentieth century scholar, the famous author of the book *Torah Tememah*, Rabbi Baruch Epstein, asked the question in his book *Baruch Sheamar*. Why do Jews begin their morning services every day with *ma tovu*, words that extol the Jews, but whose source is the non-Jewish prophet Balaam, a man who tried to curse and destroy Judaism? Isn't it inappropriate to include his words as a prayer, in the synagogue, as an introduction to the service of God? He answers simply and truthfully, the truth is the truth no matter what its source!

Personal stories

It is remarkable how people ignore this sage advice and how they choose to be ignorant rather than accept the truth from a non-Jew. Many go so far as to reject a secular education because it is primarily the views of non-Jews.

I would like to share some personal reminiscences. I grew up in Baltimore, Maryland. In the first half of the twentieth century, all the rabbis of the larger congregations, and there were quite a few, had Ph.D.s. My dad, Rabbi Dr. Nathan Drazin, received his MA in psychology from Columbia University and his Ph.D. from Johns Hopkins University. His thesis, on the *History of Jewish Education*, was published in Hebrew and in English. Being interested in study, dad acquired not only a regular ordination from Yeshiva University, but also a *semicha yadin yadin*, that authorized him to act as a judge. After serving a synagogue for 31 years, he was the president of a Baltimore Jewish day school and ended his life serving for seven years as the Director of the Institute of Judaism and Medicine in Jerusalem, making contributions to Jewish medical ethics. He used his understanding of psychology to develop the idea, later called the Baltimore plan, of making appeals for the State of Israel Bonds during the High Holiday services, thereby gaining millions of dollars for Israel. He also used this skill to write a book called *Marriage Made in Heaven*, on the problems of sex and marriage, a book published in Hebrew and in English, which saved the marriages of many observant Jews who knew very little about sex. He also wrote much on Torah. And yet when he died in 1976, rabbis suggested that his family should not include his secular title Doctor on his gravestone because it was unsuitable to mention a secular degree. We demurred.

Some time later, I was serving on a board that was looking for a rabbi at a Baltimore synagogue. The choice came down to two candidates. Both had rabbinical ordination. One had an MA from Yeshiva University and the other only had a high school education. The congregation chose the man with the high school education because they felt that the secular education of his competitor reduced his piety. The congregation later suffered because of its decision for the rabbi lacked the education, background and skills to handle a large growing congregation.

One last story. This is about a person who rejected a secular education and non-Jewish ideas simply because of their source. A Jewish high school teacher, a rabbi who refused to educate himself beyond high school, a man who was responsible for the thinking of many young people, told me that there was no need to study anything other than Jewish sources because the Talmud contains everything that one needs to know. When I pointed out that the talmudic formula for pi, the circumference of a circle, was imprecise, he responded that the Talmud is correct and science is wrong. When I told him about Maimonides' statement, he arrogantly dismissed Maimonides as mistaken.

Summary
The Torah devoted 98 verses to the non-Israelite prophet Balaam, the man who tried to curse the Israelites. The Torah does so to teach that the truth is the truth no matter its source.

The destruction of the nations of Sihon, Og and Amalek as seen in some Jewish sources

Deuteronomy 29 relates that Moses reminded the Israelites that when they approached Canaan, "Sihon, king of Heshbon, and Og, king of Bashan, went out against us in battle; we smote them, and took their land." These events are detailed in *Numbers* 21 and *Deuteronomy* 2 and 3. The battles with Heshbon and Bashan remind us of the war against Amalek in *Exodus* 17 and *Deuteronomy* 25, where the Israelites are commanded to exterminate the people.

Questions
1. What is the justification for the annihilation of Heshbon and Bashan?
2. Why were the Israelites commanded to destroy Amalek?

Heshbon and Bashan
When the Israelites were traveling in the wilderness, they sent an envoy to Sihon, king of the Amorites, with a declaration of peace and a request for permission to pass though the Amorite land. Moses assured the Amorites through his emissaries that they would keep to the road, not touch their produce and would pay for their water. Their request to Sihon and their later similar request to Og were refused, and the two nations responded with an unprovoked attack against the peaceful Israelites. The Israelites defended themselves and won the battle. They destroyed all the people and took their land.

The Jewish Greek philosopher Philo (about 20 B.C.E. to 50 C.E.) justified the Israelite behavior. He informed us that Sihon answered the envoys insolently and unjustifiably planned to kill them. He was stopped from slaughtering the messengers only because of international law respecting the treatment of envoys. Instead, he attacked the entire nation of Israel. Philo describes Sihon's Amorites as a nation sunk into the lowest levels of passion and a people who devoted themselves to corrupting truth. Thus, besides the need for defense, the extermination of the Amorites was a cauterization of a malignant and poisoning cancer. Philo does not mention Og, presumably assuming that what he said of Sihon applied to Og.

The Jewish historian and general Flavius Josephus (around 38–100 C.E.) adds further details showing the unreasonable and belligerent behavior of Sihon. Moses stated that he would agree to any terms set by Sihon and offered a commercial incentive; the Israelites would buy the Amorites' food and water and thereby enrich them. Thus there was absolutely no justification for the Amorite attack.

While the Bible seems to state that the Israelites killed all the inhabitants of these nations, neither Philo nor Josephus do so. It is possible that they recognized that the Bible frequently "speaks in human language," to quote Rabbi Ishmael, and that it sometimes exaggerates to highlight its message. Statements such as "killed all its inhabitants" should not be taken literally, as one would not take the statement, the tower of Babel "reached into the heaven" literally. The Israelites defended themselves against the unprovoked attacks of two belligerent nations and killed many of the combatants in the battle.

Amalek

While the narratives of Sihon and Og are easily understood as being reasonable, the account of Amalek is much more difficult to understand.

Exodus 17 and *Deuteronomy* 25 report that Amalek attacked the Israelites from the rear shortly after their exodus from Egypt. The Israelites defended themselves and were victorious. God commanded the Israelites through Moses to completely blot out the memory of the nation of Amalek. The command is repeated by the prophet Samuel in *I Samuel* 15. The only voice speaking against this apparent genocide is that of the first Jewish king Saul, who was strongly criticized by Samuel for not killing all of the Amalekite people and who lost his monarchy because of his apparently reasonable behavior.

Philo sidesteps the difficulty of the slaughter of an entire people by interpreting the entire report allegorically. Amalek is not a nation, but a symbol of the impassioned coward who strikes anyone he sees standing in his way. He hides until his enemy has passed him by, no longer looking at him. Then he rises and assaults what he perceives is his opponent's weakest point. Philo was thus the first to introduce the idea that it is not the people that should be eradicated, but the nefarious self destructive quality of Amalek that an individual must obliterate from his personality.

Josephus took another approach. He emphasizes that Amalek was the most war-like nation and struck the Israelites unprovoked. He states that the Bible is not commanding the Israelites to destroy Amalek, but, rather, Moses is *predicting* that Amalek will be obliterated.

Josephus justifies Samuel's command to kill the people of Amalek because they were still acting belligerently against the Israelites; and when one tries to be kind to such people, one will probably unwittingly become the begetter of further crimes. This occurred when the king of Amalek had relations with his wife during the night of his captivity, when he should have already been killed, and had a child from this union. The descendant of this child, Haman, caused the descendant of Saul, Mordechai, enormous problems. Additionally, Saul himself was later killed by the son of the Amalek king, whom he had not killed.

The Babylonian Talmud, *Yoma* 22b, seems to capture this idea. Rabbi Mani asked, how could God have commanded the obliteration of Amalek? The Talmud answers by quoting *Ecclesiastes* 7:16, "Be not righteous overmuch."

The Aramaic Bible translation known as *Pseudo-Jonathan* (generally dated in the ninth or tenth century) collects an assortment of ideas from various earlier Midrashim and elaborates imaginatively in its retelling of the Amalek story. The thrust of the targumic presentation is a picture of Amalek having an incurable long lasting hatred against Israel. Amalek was successful only when Israel sinned but lost when Israel acted properly. Thus the tale is a moral and religious lesson that encourages the Jew to behave properly. Specifically, the Amalekites, according to the Targum, were descendants of Jacob's brother Esau, and waged war against Israel simply "because of the enmity that existed between Esau and Jacob." Amalek was able to overcome some of the members of the rear tribe, that of Dan, because they were practicing idolatry and were not protected by God. Moses instructs Joshua to pick a force of men who observe the divine commandments, while he devoted himself to fasting and prayer. As long as he was involved in these activities, Israel was successful.

Some other Jewish scholars understood that the command to kill all of Amalek was not to be taken literally and not to be understood as being applicable at all times and under all circumstances. A fragment of the Dead Sea Scrolls (4Q252) seems to restrict Jews from carrying out the command to destroy Amalek until "the end of days," seemingly postponing the event until God Himself carries it out, if He wants to do so. Maimonides, in his *Mishneh Torah, Concerning Kings and Wars* 5:1 and 6:1, 4, states that Jews may not harm Amalek or any other nation during a war without first offering that they, the Jews, would cease the battle under certain circumstances. An opinion in the Babylonian Talmud, *Sanhedrin* 96b, recognized that not all Amalekite people were or should have been killed. It states that some descendants of Amalek repented, became proselytes to Judaism and studied Torah in B'nei Berak.

Summary

In sum, we see that some Jewish commentators were troubled by a literal reading of the divine command to destroy other people. We also see that they found ways to interpret and justify the incidences where a literal reading implied what they thought was cruel behavior.

Nitzavim

The dotted words

Deuteronomy 29:28 is an ambiguous sentence with dotted words. It is difficult to understand what the passage is saying. If we translate each word separately and literally, and read it without punctuations, it states: "The hidden [things belong] to the Lord our God and the revealed we and our children [must] until forever perform all the words of this Torah."

The verse has different meanings depending on where we place a semi-colon. If it is set after "revealed," the passage would say: "The hidden [things belong] to the Lord our God and the revealed; we and our children [must] until forever perform all the words of the Torah." According to this reading, God has the hidden and revealed things.

If, on the other hand, we put the semi-colon after "the Lord our God," the verse would read, "The hidden [belong] to the Lord our God; and the revealed to us and our children [must] until forever perform all the words of the Torah." In this reading, the revealed things belong to humans.

Punctuation and peculiar dotting
The verse is punctuated so that only the hidden things belong to God, but the revealed things belong to humans. Every letter of two words, *lanu*, "to us," and *u'l'vaneinu*, "and to our children," are dotted at the top, as well as the first letter of *ad*, "until."

Questions
1. What does the verse mean when it states that the hidden things belong to God?
2. Who punctuated the Torah verses?
3. When were they punctuated?
4. What is the meaning of the dots?

The Masorites

It is generally accepted that the original Torah contained no punctuations, and even no division between sentences. These were initiated by a group of people called the Masorites, a word derived from *masorah*, meaning "tradition." The Masorites did many things regarding the Torah text. There is no agreement as to when the Masorites lived. The period was probably sometime between the time of Ezra, about four centuries before the Common Era, and about the tenth century of the Common Era. There were different systems practiced by different Masoretic groups.

The punctuation served a dual purpose. It was a series of signs indicating how the text should be chanted in the Synagogue. It also indicated where there were pauses in the verse; what we would call commas, semi colons, periods, etc. Little is known about when the Masorites originated the punctuation. Mar Natronai Gaon, in the later half of the ninth century, wrote: "The punctuation was not given at Sinai. It was the sages that told us to do the punctuation." The earlier Babylonian Talmud (*Megillah* 32a, *Nedarim* 37b and *Berachot* 62a) seems to date the origin of the punctuation to the first centuries of the Common Era. However a tradition in *Megillah* 3a seems to say it was as early as the time of Ezra.

Another thing that the Masorites did was place dots in ten verses; one is the passage we are discussing. We no longer know why they did so, but there are two principle theories. One states that the dots indicate that one should give the verse or phrase special attention because it has a particularly important, sometimes hidden message. The other believes that the dots indicate that there may be some error: the word may be wrong or misplaced, the spelling may be incorrect, or, as in this case, the punctuation is suspect.

Divergent interpretations
The conservative approach

Even those who use the conservative approach disagree what the passage is stating. Rashi, taking this approach, quotes the opinion of Rabbi Nehemiah in the Babylonian Talmud, *Sanhedrin* 43b, "It is dotted over the words 'to us and to our children' to teach us that [God] did not punish society as a whole [for the misdeeds of some individual] even for things that were revealed [and clear to all], until the Israelites crossed the Jordan. At that time they accepted upon themselves by an oath on Mount Gerizim and Mount Ebal that they would be responsible for [the behavior] of each other." Rashi does not quote the opinion of Rabbi Yehuda, in the same Talmud, who states that the dots teach that the Israelites were not punished for the hidden commands until they crossed the Jordan. Rabbi Nehemiah felt, and presumably Rashi agreed, that Jews are never punished for something that is hidden from them.

One can easily see the difficulty in trying to find the special message in the dotted phrase.

1. The two talmudic scholars differed in what the dots are teaching. Thus the dots did not teach a clear lesson.

2. It is questionable whether the dotted phrase "us and our children" tell us anything about (1) punishment, (2) misdeeds of the individual being the responsibility of the many, (3) crossing the Jordan, and (4) the two mountains, as maintained by Rabbi Nehemiah. None of these items is even suggested by the wording of the sentence or the paragraph in which it appears, which discusses idol worship.

3. Rabbi Yehuda's interpretation is also questionable. The verse does not explicitly state that (1) people are punished for hidden commands, (2) why should people be punished for something they know nothing about, and (3) what is the significance of the crossing of the Jordan, which (4) is not hinted at in the verse or paragraph.

4. Even assuming that the dotted words teach the lesson the two sages indicate, why was the *ayin* of the next word *ad* dotted?

Dots indicate a suspect text

The other understanding of the dots is that it indicates a suspect text. Again there is no unanimity among those who ascribe to this method. According to this approach, although the Masorites punctuated the text as they did, they are informing us that it is possible that it could be read with the semi-colon before "us and our children." Ibn Ezra recognizes this. He states that some people try to interpret the verse contrary to the Masorite punctuation, to mean that both hidden and revealed matters belong to God, while humans have the duty to act according to Torah law. He considers this interpretation nonsense, for there is no point in mentioning it in this verse.

Chizkunee had another idea. He questioned the presence in the verse of two words rather than the punctuation. He felt that the words "to the Lord our God" are suspect, since the verse appears to have nothing to do with God. It is telling us, he writes, as Rashi states, that when the Israelites reach Canaan, they will be held responsible for the sins of others; but Rashi failed to explain why the *ayin* was dotted. He concludes that the Hebrew letters of the suspect words "to the Lord our God," total eleven. It would be improper, he continues, to place the dots over these eleven letters because a person seeing it may suppose we intend to obliterate God, so the eleven dots that belong over "to the Lord our God" are set over eleven other letters, including the *ayin*.

Interpreting without commenting on the dots

The *Targum Pseudo-Jonathan*, Ibn Ezra and Rashbam explain the biblical comment as it is punctuated, as follows: God executes judgment upon those who sin secretly, for He knows all secret things, but we (through human courts) are obligated to punish those who commit seeable wrongs.

Summary

We were introduced to the Masorites briefly and learned that, among other things, they punctuated the Torah text and dotted some words in ten verses. We saw that there were different interpretations in how the verse was punctuated. We learned about the dotting of words, and that this could alert us to search for some hidden meaning or tell us that the wording is suspect. We investigated both approaches and found that there was no agreement in how to interpret the passage by even those who agreed on the method they would use, the hidden meaning or the suspect wording. Finally, setting aside the issues of punctuation and dotting, we read a reasonable explanation of the verse presented by several commentators.

Vayeilech

What is the meaning of God predicting He will "conceal My face"?

Deuteronomy 31:17 and 18 hold an unusual, probably impossible, prediction. God informs Moses on his 120th birthday that he will die and the Israelites will "rise and stray after the idols of the foreigners of the land they are entering." God expresses His anger against the Israelites and speaks about concealing His face.

> 17. My anger will flare up against him on that day and I will forsake them. I will conceal My face from them and he will become prey. He will encounter many evils and distresses. He will say on that day, "Isn't it because my God is not with me that these evils befell me?"

> 18. Now I will definitely conceal My face on that day because of all the evil that he did, that he turned to other gods.

Questions

1. Is there any significance in Scripture changing the pronouns from the singular "him" and "he" to the plural "them?"
2. Why is it idolatry that prompts God's strong reaction?
3. Does God become angry? Doesn't anger indicate a diminishment of the divine?
4. God states that He will conceal His face. Does God have a face to conceal?
5. If God is omnipresent, meaning present everywhere, how can He conceal Himself?
6. Why would the benevolent God want to conceal Himself from the Israelites when they need Him the most?

Grammar

There are three ways commentators have answered the grammar question. First, by pointing out that the change of grammar – such as plural to singular and masculine to feminine, and the reverse – occurs very frequently in the Pentateuch, and has no significance. Second, various commentators single out some of these occurrences, but not all, and offer fanciful interpretations why Scripture made the changes. Third, sometimes a reasonable explanation is offered. Abraham ibn Ezra states here that the passage declares that God will reject all of the Israelites and each of them will suffer individually.

Idolatry

Abraham ibn Ezra comments on *Deuteronomy* 28:14 and reveals that when Jews worship idols, they are committing the worst offense, for idolatry is the root of all transgressions. Thus, it should surprise no one that when the Israelites stray to worship idols it provokes strong biblical displeasure.

Anthropomorphisms and anthropopathisms

The use of anthropomorphisms and anthropopathisms is a frequent scriptural phenomenon. Anthropomorphisms portray God performing human activities, even though God has no human body. Anthropopathisms ascribe human emotions to the divinity, even though God does not have emotions. Examples of anthropomorphisms is to say that God is talking, looking, walking, coming, going, or concealing Himself. Examples of anthropopathisms are to picture God being angry, disappointed or jealous. The Bible uses them to help people understand what is happening.

Even outside the Bible, people think of God having human physical features and human emotions because it helps them understand and to communicate to others. The Bible does so because, as Rabbi Ishmael said, "The Torah speaks in the language of people." Abraham ibn Ezra put it this way: the Torah was written for people so it had to be composed in a way they would understand, even though technically the wording is not precise.

The commentators recognize that the anthropomorphic and anthropopathic statements were not meant to be taken literally. Although they do not clarify the two sentences in detail, Saadiah explains "face" as "mercy," and Rashi reveals that "I will conceal My face" means that it will be "**as if** I do not see your distress."

Understanding verses 17 and 18

Verses 17 and 18 speak in anthropomorphic and anthropopathic figures of speech and need to be translated. The Bible is predicting that the Israelites will reject God soon after they enter Canaan, after Moses' death. The prediction is verified in the books of *Joshua* and *Judges*, where the Israelites are exposed worshipping idols and assimilating Canaanite practices.

God's "angry" reaction to this mutiny is a scriptural comment on the behavior, that it is wrong. God "concealing Himself" does not suggest that God will be doing something, but, rather, what the Israelites will do. When in *Exodus* 10:1 Scripture states that God will harden the hearts of Pharaoh and his servants, it means, as Maimonides explains in his *Guide of the Perplexed* 2:48, that the people will harden their own reactions to the Israelites, using their free will, according to God's law of nature. So, too, here, the people, not God, are concealing God from their lives by their submersion into idol worship. Maimonides' interpretation that the Egyptians, not God, hardened their hearts, is supported by the book of *Samuel* 6:6, where the Philistines, in recounting the history of Egypt, state explicitly, that the Pharaoh and his servants hardened their own hearts.

The Bible states that idol worship will have consequences. As verified in the books of *Joshua* and *Judges*, idol worship naturally led to the intermingling with the Canaanites and the adoption of some Canaanite cultural practices. The Bible is warning the Israelites that the natural consequences of such behavior will be suffering, until they reject idolatry.

An unusual interpretation

Joseph Bechor Shor gives an entirely different interpretation of the two sentences. They, in his opinion, are foretelling that God will ultimately save the Jews, and the wording gives the date that the salvation will occur. He derives the date by the use of *gematria*, examining the numerical value of the Hebrew letters in the words. Thus, *aleph* is one, *bet* is two, *gimmel* is three, etc. The rationalist Abraham ibn Ezra derided the sport of *gematria* saying in his commentary to *Exodus* 1:7, "God forbid that a prophet should communicate with *gematria*."

Summary

Deuteronomy 31:17 and 18 prompted the introduction of many ideas. It showed examples of the Bible changing tenses, and three methods of understanding this phenomenon were mentioned. Idolatry was identified as the fundamental evil that removes one from God and has dire consequences. Anthropomorphisms and anthropopathisms were seen as frequently occurring biblical usages that must not be taken literally. The Bible uses them freely to communicate easily, but they must be understood in a way that does not ascribe human features and emotions to God. One commentator interpreted the two sentences by using *gematria*, but this method or sport of seeking meaning in the numerical value of letters was derided by another commentator.

Haazinu

Moses' last words

Deuteronomy 32:47 and 33:29 contain Moses' final words. In verse 32:47, Moses assures his people that the Torah is important and that it will benefit them, "For it is not an empty thing for you, it is your life; with this thing you will prolong your life on the land to which you are crossing the Jordan to possess." The Bible then records Moses blessing the people. Moses concludes with a similar statement in 33:29, "Israel, you are fortunate; who is like you, a nation delivered by the Lord, the shield of your help, the sword of your greatness; your foes may try to deceive you, but you will tread upon their high places."

Questions
1. What is the value of Torah?
2. What is the meaning of, "For it is not an empty thing for you"?
3. Is Moses' last words related to the first teaching of the Torah, that one must use one's intelligence in all ways, including how one interprets the Torah?
4. Does Maimonides, who stressed that the introduction of the Bible teaches people to use their intelligence, see the idea reiterated in Moses' final statement?

A parable
The second century Greek historian Plutarch told the following story in his life of Publicola (Loeb Classical Library, pages 555–557). "They say that all Greek doors used to open outward... where those who are about to go out of a house beat noisily on the inside of their own doors, in order that persons passing by or standing in front of them may hear, and not be taken by surprise when the doors open out into the street."

As Moses was about to depart this world, he metaphorically knocked on the door, alerted his people that he was leaving, and expressed concern for their safety. He told them his final message. He addressed the quality of the Torah and how it affects their lives.

Maimonides' interpretation

Maimonides understood that Moses' final message was the same important concept that he saw in the introduction to the Torah. In the first chapter of his *Guide of the Perplexed,* he interpreted the terms "God's image" and "God's form" in the first chapter of *Genesis* to teach people that they have a divine gift of intelligence and are obligated to gain knowledge and use their minds. He reads this lesson into the words of *Deuteronomy* 32:47, "For it is not an empty thing for you, it is your life."

In 3:26 of his *Guide,* he emphasizes that all of God's actions have a reason and usefulness. God does not issue commands that are arbitrary. He mentions that some people are unable to understand some commands, and comments, "our sages generally do not think that such precepts have no cause whatever, and serve no purpose; for this would lead us to assume that God's actions are purposeless." The reason we do not understand some commands is simply "owing either to the deficiency of our knowledge or the weakness of our intellect." The reasons for the commands would be known if we work to gain knowledge. A person who understands the purpose of the commands can do more good for himself and society.

Maimonides sees that Moses is making this point when he tells the people, "For it is not an empty thing for you." He understands the statement, "For it [meaning, as the prior verses make clear, the Torah] is not an empty thing," as: it is not devoid of reason. He reads "for you" separately, as "it is only through you." He explains, "This means that the giving of these commandments is not an empty thing and without any useful purpose. If any command appears so to you, it is because of the deficiency in your comprehension." Maimonides then continues his *Guide* with an explanation of all of the commands.

He ends his *Guide* as Moses ended his statements to his people, encouraging them to realize that the world was created with wisdom, people should not back away from thinking, and human and societal perfection comes through knowledge.

The object (of what I said is) to declare that the perfection in which a person can truly glory is obtained when the person acquires – as much as a human is able – knowledge of God, knowledge of how He interacts with this world, and how humans are impacted in what they do and how they live. Once this knowledge is acquired, the person will be determined to seek loving-kindness, justice and righteousness always.

Summary

Like the beginning of the Bible, Moses ends his leadership by cautioning his people to remember the importance of attaining knowledge and to use this knowledge in all things. Knowledge will lead to the perfection of the individual and society. Torah contains this knowledge because it is a compilation of divine commands, all of which are based on good and useful reasoning. Indeed, as the 32:47 continues, "it is your life."

Vezot Haberachah

Ibn Ezra's "Secret of the Twelve"

The Torah's final chapter presents a serious theological dilemma. The following is a brief history of how some scholars handled this dilemma.

Questions
1. Did Moses write the entire Torah?
2. Do traditional Jewish commentators differ on the subject?

Who wrote the story of the death of Moses?
The twelve verses of *Deuteronomy* chapter 34 tell the story of the death of Moses. The introductory four verses narrate how God told Moses to ascend Mount Nebo. He showed Moses the land He had promised Abraham, Isaac and Jacob that He would give to their descendants. The final eight verses begin with the statement that Moses died there and continues with facts that occurred after his death. He was buried there after living 120 years, the Israelites mourned him for thirty days, Joshua succeeded him, and no prophet arose after him that was like him.

Is it a principle of Jewish belief that Moses wrote the entire Torah?
The usual understanding of Jewish tradition is that Moses wrote the entire Torah. In his *Introduction to Chelek*, Maimonides (1138–1204) lists thirteen fundamental principles of Judaism. The eighth is that the entire Torah that we possess today was given by God to Moses. It is true that many Maimonidean scholars such as Yeshayahu Leibowitz, in his series of books on the *Guide of the Perplexed*, claims that Maimonides himself did not believe this principle and most of the other thirteen. He writes that Maimonides included this idea for the sake of the masses, just as he included many other statements in his writings for this purpose. Be this as it may, traditional Jews, even as Leibowitz admits, believe that the entire Torah was given to the Israelites by God through

Moses. But since chapter 34 deals with Moses' death and its aftermath, how could Moses write about his death and what occurred afterwards?

Rashi quotes the Talmud and Midrash

The question is an old one. Rashi, the foremost Bible commentator of the eleventh century, summarizes the responses contained in the Babylonian Talmud, *Bava Batra* 15a and *Menachot* 30a, and the *Midrash Sifre*.

> Is it possible that Moses wrote "and Moses died there"? But, Moses wrote until this verse (verse 5) and afterwards Joshua wrote. (This was the opinion of Rabbi Yehuda or Rabbi Nehemiah. However, Rabbi Meyer felt that Moses wrote the entire Torah.)... The Holy One, blessed be He, spoke, and Moses wrote with tears.

Abraham ibn Ezra

The first opinion, that Moses did not write the entire Torah opened a Pandora's Box. Realizing that Moses was on top of the mountain where he died and did not descend to report what happened there even before he died, the twelfth century commentator Abraham ibn Ezra states that Moses did not write all twelve passages in this chapter. He suggests that the chapter was written by Joshua who knew what occurred through prophecy.

While this seems innocuous, it is actually part of a general concept of ibn Ezra that he calls the "secret of the twelve." He seems to contend that just as these twelve verses were not written by Moses, so too there are other passages that Moses did not write. Since most people could not or would not accept this idea, he decided to keep it a secret.

Ibn Ezra is one of the foremost traditional Bible commentators. His commentary is printed with those of other traditional Bible commentators in the "Rabbinic Bibles" and is frequently quoted from synagogue pulpits. Yet, he is one of the most rationalistic Bible commentators and many who read his views for the first time are surprised at its content.

Ibn Ezra's secret of the twelve

Ibn Ezra mentions his "secret of the twelve" in his commentary to *Deuteronomy* 1:2. The "secret" is not spelled out in any detail, probably because of his fear of offending those with a contrary view. It is explained by ibn Ezra's super commentator Josef Bonfils in his *Zophnat Panei'ach,* which he wrote in 1370. Ibn Ezra lists six biblical passages that he felt could not have been composed by Moses.

1. *Deuteronomy* 1:1 relates that God spoke to Moses on the "other side of the Jordan." This implies that the writer wrote from the eastern side of the Jordan, but Moses never crossed the Jordan.

2. *Deuteronomy* 31:9 uses the third person "and Moses wrote." This seems to indicate that some other writer is narrating the deeds and writings of Moses.

3. *Genesis* 12:6 recites that Abraham traveled throughout the land of Canaan. It adds "and the Canaanite was then in the land." The statement appears to exclude the time when the passage was written when Canaanites were no longer in the land. Therefore it must have been composed after Moses' death, after the Canaanites had been driven from Canaan.

4. *Genesis 22:14* calls Mount Moriah the mount of God. Since the mountain probably did not acquire this name until after the building of the Temple on this site, the choice of the Temple site was not made during Moses' lifetime, and Moses did not indicate any spot chosen by God, the phrase must have been composed many years after Moses' death.

5. *Deuteronomy* 3:11 states that the bed of Og, king of Bashan, was nine cubits long and four cubits wide. Since the bed was probably not discovered until the city of Rabbath, where it was located, was conquered by David, it could not have been written before the Davidic era.

6. *Deuteronomy* 27:1 reports that the entire Torah was written on stones and the rabbis explain that there were twelve stones. Ibn Ezra remarks, if Moses wrote all of the material that we consider the Torah today, it could not be placed on only twelve stones.

It is of course true that one could explain each of the half dozen passages mentioned by ibn Ezra and show that they do not necessarily imply that Moses did not write them. Indeed, the Talmuds address and answer these and similar problems and many later Torah scholars wrote explanations. However, ibn Ezra himself felt that they prove that Moses did not write the entire Torah.

Baruch Spinoza

In 1670, Baruch de Spinoza (1634–1677) – who was excommunicated for his beliefs – published his *Tractatus Theologico-Publicus* and took the expected next step. He mentions the passages that ibn Ezra noted and writes that while the "secret of the twelve" could refer to the last twelve verses of the Pentateuch, it could also refer to the twelve stone tablets, which suggest that Moses' Torah was far smaller than the Pentateuch we have today. He contends that ibn Ezra must have noted many more passages that show that Moses did not compose them. He lists about another half dozen passages of this type and concludes: "From what has been said, it is clearer than the sun at noonday that the Pentateuch was not written by Moses, but by someone who lived long after him."

Summary

The story of the death of Moses raises the question, did Moses write the entire Pentateuch? The Talmud and Midrash have two opinions, yes and no. Maimonides is obscure and can be interpreted both ways. Ibn Ezra clearly did not believe that the entire Torah was written by Moses, although he does not state his opinion openly. He mentions about a half dozen verses that indicate to him that they could not have been authored while Moses was alive. Spinoza insisted that ibn Ezra would agree with his own view that more verses than he mentioned were also not composed by Moses.

About the Author

Rabbi Dr. Israel Drazin has been successful in several significant fields. He is a noted Bible scholar, an author of ten books, a United States Army Brigadier General and chaplain, a rabbi and a lawyer.

As a lawyer, he headed the United States' Medicare's civil litigation staff. In the United States Army, General Drazin developed the legal argument that saved the military chaplaincies of the Army, Navy and Air Force when lawyers insisted in court that these institutions were a violation of the First Amendment to the US Constitution.

Seven of his ten books are on Targum Onkelos, the fourth century Aramaic translation of the Pentateuch. By careful analysis of the ten thousand differences between the wording of the Targum and the Bible, Dr. Drazin was the first scholar who was able to identify the date of the Targum. He showed the Targum's consistent reliance on the final edited version of the tannaitic Midrashim – which were edited around 400 CE – and that the Aramaic translator even copied a version of the Hebrew words of the Midrashim hundreds of times into his Aramaic translation.

Dr. Drazin received his Rabbinic Ordination in 1957 from the Ner Israel Yeshiva in Baltimore, Maryland.